ALL ABOUT THE MONEY

BEING OLD AND BROKE STINKS

A SIMPLE GUIDE TO INVESTING AND
FINANCIAL KNOW-HOW

KIRK D.ALLEN

KIRK D.ALLEN

ISBN:1530441285
ISBN-13:9781530441280

DEDICATION

I dedicate to my family, friends and readers.

CONTENTS

ACKNOWLEDGMENTS

Thank you my wonderful editor. You're an incredible person! I could not have brought this to life without your assistance!

INTRODUCTION

The inception of my financial
knowledge became most palpable during
the summer of my thirteenth birthday.
My Uncle Manley and Aunt Mervis had no
children and would visit my home,
gladly bestowing gifts and money on me
as if I were their own child. The
spring season of my thirteenth
birthday, I received a personal
invitation to visit Boston,
Massachusetts where I would earn some

cash working in one of my uncle's stores and have an overall great time. I knew I was going to work but surely the promise of extras, the trip to the aquarium, a new bike, clothes, toys, a boom box, and a Walkman (dual side cassette playing capability) would make this the best summer ever!

My first day in Boston was fantastic and it was capped off by eating dinner at a fancy five star restaurant. I did not have the proper attire, which Aunt Mervis remedied via a quick shopping jaunt. I was thinking, this is not bad at all (I needed something and I immediately got it). I quickly took note of how my aunt and uncle seldom ate at home. Week nights equated to "dress to impress"; we were going out to a rather nice restaurant. Lunch was less formal but lunch was prepared by someone other than my aunt and uncle, and had a price tag.

ALL ABOUT THE MONEY

Uncle Manley and Aunt Mervis also enjoyed their cars. Multiple cars littered the driveway, far more than the two-car garage could hold. I assumed when people owned a gigantic home they needed to have lots of cars.

Shopping was a daily activity, apparently their lifestyle demands lavishing gifts on family and friends. Dinner tabs fell into my uncle's court (or out of my uncle's fairly over stuffed wallet), and was greeted with outward smiles and inner applause by all who enjoyed the meal.

My aunt left her job, as a nurse, since the stores were doing exceptionally well. Occasionally, she would visit the stores helping out in some capacity; however, most times it was to relieve me from work for the rest of the day. We'd leave and do cool things like sightseeing and visiting the aquarium. I really enjoyed seeing the sharks. The best was seeing the hammerhead shark swim right up to the glass, it was so exhilarating seeing such a fantastic animal up close.

Life is funny; if you do something well, people notice and they may emulate exactly what you're doing. Individuals who pay little or no attention to competition join the ranks of the dodo bird - extinction!

Uncle Manley and Aunt Mervis spent money as if the source was a never ending stream. My uncle was not prepared for competition or perhaps he realized too late that his business was declining. Time forced Uncle Manley to close his stores as competitors drew away customers.

My uncle thought the good times would never end. Now late in his 50's, he had to restart. No savings! No pension! Aunt Mervis returned to nursing and worked until the day she died. Uncle Manley, try as he might, could not restart a business to resemble anything close to what he had previously.

He now spends his days in a less than desirable government nursing home, scratching by on Social Security. My uncle was extremely popular as long as the money was flowing; however, when his money dried up so too did his parasitic friends and leech-like family members.

The good times ended with a thud! I vowed not to be my spend-aholic uncle. Tomorrow may appear to be a million miles away, but it has a funny way of sneaking up on you.

The world has grown more sophisticated and has far greater understanding (and perhaps fear) of the markets. My goal is to inform readers with simple possible life-helping ideas, and suggestions.

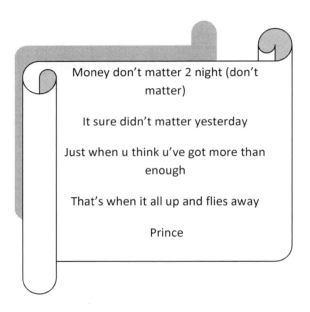

Money don't matter 2 night (don't matter)

It sure didn't matter yesterday

Just when u think u've got more than enough

That's when it all up and flies away

Prince

Bottom line – I am *here* to keep it simple with straight talk and common sense financial wisdom. Money! I'm all about the money! My money! Your money! Money is central! We need to earn money, investment money, and have it last as long as we do.

It is my inconvertible belief you will benefit from the ideas,

philosophies and interviews I've
managed to put together in this
book. I am certain that anyone who
reads my book will walk away with
knowledge to navigate through
current and future financial
decisions. Welcome to the beginning
of questions and the road to
answers. This is the inauguration
of a prosperous financial outcome.
Enjoy.

Kirk Allen

Hello

"Sometimes you gotta go back to the beginning to learn" Kenny Parker

ALL ABOUT THE MONEY

Pick a number, any number. Okay, let me make it more specific. Pick a dollar amount, any dollar amount. So if you had this realistic amount of money all would be well in your world? This is not a **Houdini** moment. I will not tell you the number you have chosen. Here is what I'm going to tell you-my number. My number is the greatest number ever conceived in origin of great numbers. Freedom begins with mastering this number. Governments comprised of abundant brilliant humanistic individuals quarrel **ad infinitum** on the various ways to reach this number. Do not attempt to guess my number. My number is zero!

Zero! Hell yes, zero! Now that you think I'm crazy allow me a moment to explain myself. Individuals who are buried beneath mountains of bills, loans, credit cards, mortgage, medical bills, car related bills, alimony, child support, and so forth understand the thought of owing no one and residing at zero. These items keep people up at night causing stress and distress simply because they reside beneath the zero threshold. They live in a world funded, controlled, manipulated, and navigated by the various vehicles of debt which keep them below zero. Sure they have a couple of bucks in the bank, but if they liquidated all their assets and paid every penny toward their debt they still would remain beneath zero.

Those above zero have little to no debt. Their debt load is temporary. For them, debt elimination is a means of writing a check, pressing a button, or handing cash or cash equivalents to the debt owner. Escaping from subzero is a mere act of simplicity and easy kinesthetic. Individuals at zero or above, whether it is one cent or one billion dollars, may not sleep in the same type of bed, but they sleep far better than someone who is attempting to escape the realm of debt. Go ahead dream of millions of dollars, dream of billions of dollars, but first work, endeavor and fight to reach zero. I promise nothing regarding eternal bliss, perfect health or a perfect family. However, wouldn't life be better if you didn't have to worry about paying X Y and Z?

First A Bit Of Advice: Don't "Act"

Avoid the urge to 'act'. It is fair to say we all know someone that is living the 'act' lifestyle. This person will 'act' like they can afford the mini mansion. This person will 'act' like they can afford the luxury car. This person will 'act' like they can afford the designer clothes. This person will 'act' like they can afford the jewelry, and designer bags. This person will 'act' like they can afford the vacation. This person will 'act' their way into huge debt. Don't 'act'!

There are so many reasons why I feel financial education is paramount in today's world.   I can recall thousands conversations with my cousin Noel regarding our current and future financial outlook.   I can recount hundreds of finance related text messages between myself and my good friend Fyffe. Last but surely not least my niece Ana always has brigade of questions concerning financial awareness. The greatest quests are often those conceived within realm of attaining pure and unstained knowledge. This financial pilgrimage is mine

journey into a world often ignored.
People to frequently realize the
importance financial health after an
event has severely hampered finances or
activated damaged which have exceed
financial healing. This endeavor was my
financial vision quests and I have
chosen to share it with all who wonder
or thirst for financial knowledge.
The article below encompasses many of
the queries asked by friends and
family. The following article reflects
my concerns and echoes observations of
my family, and my friends.

Fast Facts

Shocking number of Americans have no
retirement savings

"Much has been written about the
"sandwich generation" -- middle-aged
Americans who are caught between their
financial obligations to elderly
parents and to their children, while
they also try to prepare for their own
retirement years. Yet millions of
Americans face an even bigger bind:
More than one-third of all working-age
adults haven't managed to save any
money toward retirement, according to a
new survey by Bankrate.com. The
personal finance site found that 26
percent of people 50-to-54-year-olds
and 14 percent of those age 65 and
older have no savings. The survey of
over 1,000 adults living across the
U.S. also found that 69 percent of 18-
to-29-year-olds and a third of 30-to-49
year-olds have yet start putting
something away for their later years.

The Bankrate findings jibe with other research that illustrate the <u>dearth of retirement savings</u>. The median retirement account balance for all working-age households in the U.S. is $3,000, and $12,000 for near-retirement households, according to the National Institute on Retirement Security. The news isn't all bad. Those who are saving for retirement are starting earlier than in the past. And Millennials -- people born between 1980 ad 2000 -- at least feel more financially secure than any other age group surveyed, which may account for their lack of retirement savings. Of course, preparing for retirement in a post-recession economy is <u>easier said than done</u>. A recent <u>CBS News poll</u> found that about 70 percent of working Americans are finding it hard to save for retirement at all, as they attempt to pay bills and meet their basic living expenses. Only 18 percent of U.S. workers say they are very

confident of having enough money to
live comfortably during their
retirement years, according to the
Employee Benefit Research Institute."
http://www.cbsnews.com/news/shocking-
number-of-americans-have-no-retirement-
savings/

There is a startling fact that
crossed my path. It revolves around a
few hundred dollars. How incredibly
troubling would it be if the moment of
need arrived and you had less than $500
to help yourself or your family? The
obvious answer is a deep feeling of
regret mixed with lots of "why didn't I
prepare for the unexpected events in
life?" **"Close to half have no cash
savings and are living on the edge of
financial disaster, according to a
recent CreditDonkey.com survey. While
59% of respondents reported having more**

**than $500 in savings, the other 41% do
not have a cash safety net."
http://www.creditdonkey.com/no-
emergency-savings.html**

Where you are right now and where
you will be varies based on a few
important factors. First and foremost,
how old are you? Age of an investor,
age of debtor, age of someone who just
wants more money or age of someone who
wants debt reduction is extremely
important. The younger you start
investing, the better off you are.
Young investors can take risks. They
are afforded the luxury of time. Older
investors are not as fortunate with
time. There is a bit of Dorian Gray in
most people - their thinking is, "Hey,
I won't die I'll live forever." Guess
what? They never do.

There's an old belief that midlife
crisis appears during a person's 50's.
Perhaps that's a reach unless you're
assured of living to 110 years old.

The numbers say a fair percentage of us living today will even sniff 100 years old. However with good genetics, exercise, diet, proper sleep, some luck and non-Stephen King scenarios causing something crazy to happen to your car, home, family, neighbor, or local pizza delivery pimpled-faced teen, 80 years of age is not a an impossible leap. Assume you are currently your in 40's; say hello to midlife crisis or deny it. If you are younger than 40 years old time is on your side.

Time and a healthy life are something we all want more of and something most of us would gladly pay to extend as long as possible. Imagine if someone knocked on your front door and said, "Good evening. I'm from the Extend Your Time on Earth Company and I would like to offer you the chance to extend your life. How does an additional six months, a year, five years sound?" How would you respond?

ALL ABOUT THE MONEY

What if extended life came in a pill, a drink, or a meal? How many of us would jump at the opportunity?

Productive time is not infinite. Therefore, it is essential to maximize financial growth during your most productive time. You cannot negotiate to regain lost time. However, by starting at an early age, time will not snicker as you scramble in your quinquagenarian and **sexagenarian y**ears. There will come a day when you will say, *"That's it. I am out of here" to your occupation*. Individuals who can picture the end of their working days, and are prepared, have a supreme partner in the form of time. Willingness to conspire with time has given them a sense of freedom most people lack. I will regale the concrete impact time will administer to the numbers you can acquire in your investment life as we move on.

Very few individuals know exactly

what they want to be when they grow up. At some point in my younger days I wanted to be an actor, comedian, a professional baseball player, Olympic athlete, bantamweight boxer, a corporate lawyer, secret agent, politician, and the list goes on and on.

To be honest, growing up I only knew one person from fourth grade on who knew exactly what they wanted to be: my friend Dave Magill. Dave wanted to work as a train engineer. College wasn't something he wanted any part of; he did, however, attend community college to please his parents. Try as they might, his parents could not dissuade his goal of being an engineer for Amtrak, Conrail, or whoever would give him a shot at realizing his dream. I can recall a conversation where his dad said, "I don't care if you get a degree in basket weaving!" I can honestly say at one point I thought

Dave was crazy. Dave stuck to his guns and attended community college but his dream was realized through persistence. I'm very happy to say today my friend Dave is a train engineer making a fantastic living, married to a beautiful lady, and raising their baby girl.

Your choice of occupation, or the one that chooses you, will greatly enhance your present and future lifestyle. Let's face it-minimum wage workers do not take frequent vacations. Minimum wage workers are not likely to engage in the following based observation of family, friends and my community:

✓ **take trips requiring a passport**
✓ **take trips which necessitate the use of another language**
✓ **take trips across the country**
✓ **take resort-stay trips**
✓ **take weekends trips to the private lake house**

They may do this if they save for a long period of time or go into huge debt. The more money you make, the better trips you will take and that's just a fact. The more money you make, the more you can invest towards your retirement.

The more money you make, the easier it is to move on from financial management errors such as: buying an expensive watch, purse, shoe, spending way too much money hanging with friends in Las Vegas, all of which can lead to regret. However, if you make $75,000 per year, it may be easy to chalk it up as a one time poor decision: a moment of high living and debauchery. I chose $75,000 because of an article I read and it's quite a bit of money. "The Wall Street Journal: The Perfect Salary for Happiness: $75,000" http://blogs.wsj.com/wealth/2010/09/07/the-perfect-salary-for-happiness-75000-a-year

ALL ABOUT THE MONEY

Minimum wage may not provide the financial escape route for those earners to recover from bad decisions in a short period of time. Their recovery may be a day-to-day struggle for those individuals not fortunate enough to command a fast-paced recovery that an income-generating profession affords.

We just spoke about time. Time will end for all of us. We will leave behind people we love and are devoted to and can't imagine living without. How do we protect those we leave behind? How do we care for those we leave behind? There will no longer be physical reassurance. There is no hand left for them to hold, or shoulder left for them to cry on. There is no more you to support those who need you. There is a protector of sorts, life insurance! Yes, life insurance. It really should be called the following:

✓ **Death insurance**

- ✓ **Got hit by a truck insurance**
- ✓ **Choked on a piece of fruit insurance**
- ✓ **Terrible car accident insurance**
- ✓ **Dating the crazy person ran me down in the parking lot insurance**
- ✓ **Hanging with my troubled cousin got and shot insurance**

Somehow I think the commercial viability of insurance would not be as prominent if they said that in the media.

I hung out a few times with a cousin of mine in my teen years and there were times when life insurance might have been a good buy. We were shot at three times! I should say he was shot at three times when I was with him and he was shot countless more when I wasn't with him. Hence, I did not hang with him that much. He's definitely lucky (or the shooters were just terrible shots). Insurance commercials would not be as appealing if the former scenarios were used.

Imagine a commercial saying:

- ✓ **So you think your co-worker is psychotic! You better get co-worker goes on a shooting spree life insurance!**
- ✓ **Seldom chew your food? Talking while eating then choking to death insurance is for you!**
- ✓ **Constantly distracted while driving or find it difficult to stay awake while driving? Car death insurance is for you!**

Has a nice ring to it right? I would find it very difficult to let the insurance salesperson in the front door, and invite them to sit at the dining table.

Life insurance has a huge tax benefit for the large amounts of money which are passed on to the beneficiaries. Life insurance is one of the few things the federal and state governments do not tax (and I hope this will never change). Having life insurance will aid your family not only in your burial, but in paying for home, car, college, basic needs and beyond, based on the amount received. My friend Ken refuses to get life insurance because he feels this is a precursor to an early demise. He feels signing the paper for life insurance equates to the Grim Reaper knocking on your door. He also feels people will instantly hire a hit man and take you out. I felt differently. I explained it to Ken this way; I want my family not to have a huge reduction in their lifestyle. My family remains in the home, kids can go to college, and lingering debt can be dismantled. The best part of all, is that the next woman or man can move into your home, replace all of your pictures with theirs, and know you've provided a financially stable situation for them. They might even say, "thanks pal."

Credit

"In our country (Jamaica) we do credit or debit — but we favor cash!" Kes

Spending Tip

Want to control your spending? Are you sure? Well give yourself fewer credit card options. Forget about carrying as many cards as a Las Vegas Poker Dealer. Be brave and live with a maximum of two cards if you need the comfort of more than one. Here's the trick; carry one credit card and when it's necessary to use a credit card use only that one. Rid yourself of the store cards, the gas card and all other cards with interest rates nearing 18%. The APR could be less, but if someone has bad credit, which is tied to a low credit score, you can expect the APR to be fairly high. APR is the Annual Percentage Rate. There is a direct correlation between APR and credit score. This is the interest rate you will be charged for the loan over a year's time. The lower the APR, the better your credit score is; conversely, the better your credit score is, the lower the APR.

Things which may help your credit score:

1. Do not carry all your cards with you
2. Use cards only when necessary
3. Pay bills on time
4. Pay more than the minimum payment
5. Check monthly statements
6. Use cards only in places you trust
7. Avoid using your cards to acquire cash (cash withdrawals from ATMs are often more costly than traditional credit card purchases)
8. Use cards wisely when ordering items or services online
9. Hide cards when watching online shopping networks
10. Do not allow anyone to haphazardly use your cards

Let's play Poker. What do you call a hand with two Visas, two American

Express cards, and a Master Card? It's not a full house. It's a broken house or a home in debt. I'm sure if you're sauntering around with a wallet or purse such as, Fendi, Coach, Louis Vuitton, Gucci, Jimmy Choo, Michael Kors, you look fantastic. Compliments abound as onlookers and passersby's are filled with jealousy as someone so nattily kitted out must be wealthy. Yet are you empty inside? Not you personally but the bags. Perhaps they are filled with loads of credit cards with tremendous debt.

Rose, a friend I had years ago, was drop-dead gorgeous. Rose was always impeccably dressed, accessories were of Italian and other European origins, shoes were Asian, all her electronic gadgets were named after a fruit, makeup was top of the line. She once told me she would rather have all the best clothes, bags, shoes, car and jewelry and no food at home. I asked if she was serious. She said yes (we soon thereafter ended our friendship). The cost of aiding her to carry on her charade was more than I could handle.

I know couples with fantastic homes in great neighborhoods but they struggle to pay their mortgages. They struggled to pay for those cars which made people notice them every single moment they dove. These individuals survive on credit cards. ***"While the numbers vary, in general, across the board, Americans have anywhere between 4 and 10 credit cards in their wallet! (Among other issues for those with ten credit cards is finding a wallet with that many slots for cards!) This amounts to around $8,000 to $10,000 in credit card debt alone, and has nothing whatever to do with money owed in car or house payments."*** ***How Many Credit Cards does the Average American Have?*** http://www.gettingacreditcard.com/article57.shtml

Daniel P. Ray's stories at CreditCards.com

Mr. Ray delivers facts and figures regarding the use, misuse and tendencies of credit card holders. No one is inoculated with a weaken serum of bad credit vaccine as toddler which prevents idiotic, foolhardy, senseless credit actions.

✓ **Women are more likely than men to carry a credit card balance, make the minimum payment on their credit cards and be charged a late fee.**

✓ **Males who carried a credit card balance as of April 2012: 55 percent.**

✓ **Females who carried a credit card balance as of April 2012: 60 percent.**

✓ **Among men and women with low levels of financial literacy, women are likely to engage in significantly more costly behaviors than men.**

✓ **Among men and women with high levels of financial literacy there are no differences in behavior between the sexes.**

Credit card statistics, industry facts, debt statistics by Daniel P. Ray and Yasmin Ghahremani

http://www.creditcards.com/credit-card-news/credit-card-industry-facts-personal-debt-statistics-1276.php

Recall the story of the emperor and his clothes? You know, he thought he had the finest tailored suit ever made for which he paid a fortune. So the day came when the vain emperor went to show his loyal subjects his latest outfit. He walked through the streets of his kingdom and everyone was in awe of his fine attire all save one - a child who noticed he was naked. Are you the naked emperor? Are you deeply concerned about monthly credit card bills? Each month are these bills increasingly becoming a larger portion of your net monthly pay?

People, it is time for a moment of clarity. Do you know exactly what a credit card is? Do you know what a charge card is? Do you know what finance charges are? Well, let's dig into that right now. Visa, MasterCard, American Express, Discover J.C. Penny's, Macy's, Banana Republic are forms of credit cards and charge cards. Credit cards allow the user, usually 18 or older, to purchase goods or pay for services whenever they want, and wherever these cards are accepted. These cards can be used via personal contact with the merchant, over the phone, via the Internet, smart phones, and old reliable mail order.

Financial institutions issue a credit card to an individual giving them the ability to use the credit card as they see fit wherever the credit card is accepted. Companies may charge a fee for the privilege of carrying their card; however, their money makers are interest rate charges and additional fees for late payments or surpassing the maximum credit amount allotted. Most credit card users do not pay entire balances immediately when the bill is due. They will pay the minimum or perhaps slightly more than the minimum. Therefore, interest will accrue on the remaining balance, thereby providing the credit card company with a source of income and the user with the ability to use the card once more as long as the permitted loan amount has not been exceeded.

Maureen has a credit limit of $5000 and charges $1000. When Maureen receives her monthly bill she will pay $500. Maureen can still charge over $4000. A late fee will be assessed if Maureen pays her bill on the 25th of June because the payment was due on the

19th of June. Late Fees (penalties) can be $20, $25, $30 or greater. The exact amount is written on the bill or application you failed to read.

What is a charge card? Charge cards generally do not strap the holder with a preconceived limit on spending. Spend as you wish, but beware when the bill comes due. The entire bill is due. Maureen charges $1,000, Maureen must pay $1,000. The best example of a late charge card is the American Express Card.

Consolidation is one of the first steps toward controlling one's debt. Consolidating credit cards simply means you will no longer use 3, 4, 5, 6 cards and you will no longer pay each month on 3, 4, 5, 6 cards. You will pay one payment to one credit card company with one interest rate charged to one card. Consolidation; or balance transfer; may provide you with a deal from six months to a year of lower interest rate based on the credit card company you are working with.

Realize you should always endeavor to pay more than the minimum payment on credit card debt. Maureen decides to only pay the minimum on a $2,000 credit card balance. She pays on time month after month year after year. Maureen is a great client for the credit card company. At this rate Maureen will take almost twenty years to rid herself of this albatross of debt payments netting the credit card company $3,800 in profits. Total repayment amount $5,800. Friends, this is way too much time and money. The issuing company will appreciate your generosity in helping to continuously increase their bottom line. Money wasted!

"It could take a very long time to pay off your credit card if you only pay the minimum amount on your monthly credit card bill. Also, you'll end up paying more because of accumulating

interest charges. The minimum payment is the minimum amount you can pay to keep the account from going into default and incurring fees and penalties. Most card issuers require a minimum payment of 2% of the outstanding balance or $10, whichever is higher**." Credit Card Repayment Table How long will it take to pay off your credit card?
http://www.aie.org/managing-your-money/credit-cards/The-True-Cost-of-Credit-Cards-A-Repayment-Table.cfm

Balance	$1000	$2000	$3000	$4000	$5000
Interest Rate	Years to Pay Off at 2% Minimum Payment[1]				
10%	10.4	15.3	18.3	20.3	21.8
11%	11.0	16.3	19.4	21.6	23.3
12%	11.7	17.4	20.8	23.2	25.0
13%	12.4	18.7	22.3	24.9	26.9
14%	13.3	20.2	24.3	27.1	29.3
15%	14.3	22.0	26.5	29.7	32.2
16%	15.6	24.3	29.3	32.9	35.7
17%	17.3	27.1	32.9	37.0	40.2
18%	19.3	30.9	37.6	42.4	46.1
19%	22.3	36.1	44.2	*	*
20%	26.4	43.7	*	*	*
21%	46.1	*	*	*	*
22%	*	*	*	*	*
23%	*	*	*	*	*
24%	*	*	*	*	*
25%	*	*	*	*	*
26%	*	*	*	*	*
27%	*	*	*	*	*
28%	*	*	*	*	*

Extra! Extra! Read all about it! The time-honored cry of newspaper boys from the 1890's to the 1940's meant something major had occurred and it was a must read. Credit card payers should also shout, "Extra, Extra!" Each month there should be a payment above the required minimum payment. Looking for a magic dollar amount above the minimum payment? I can't say what that amount is, but let's just say if the amount above the minimum does not impede on how one eats or on your ability to acquire necessities for living - that is your magic number.

"The key to success is having a plan of how and when you'll pay off debt. For example, by paying an extra $25 to $50 a month toward one of your credit card bills, you'll be able to pay off that card and then move to the next one. Consider the example of a $2,000 balance at 18% interest.

✓ **If your minimum payment is 2% of the balance due each month, it will take you about 19 years to pay it off and you'll pay $3,862 in interest. (A 2% minimum payment would start at $40 and taper to $20. Maintain the $40 and you'll pay off the debt faster. That's what our calculator assumes.)**

✓ **If you're paying 4% of the balance due, you'll pay off the balance in seven years and four months, and you'll cut**

your interest costs to $1,031. (A 4%
minimum payment starts at $80 and
tapers to $20.)

✓ By paying 8% of the balance due—much
more than the minimum—it will take you
three years and nine months to pay it
off, and you'll pay about $433 in
interest. (An 8% minimum payment starts
at $160 and tapers to $20.)"
Calculator: How Can I Pay Off Debt
Credit Card Debt
http://planit.cuna.org/015111/article.p
hp?doc_id=40

A few quick credit card tips:

- Call your credit card company and ask
  for a lower interest rate. Tell them
  you'll cancel the card if they don't
  reduce the interest rate. If they balk
  at the request, find another credit
  card company with a better rate.
- Check your credit report periodically.

- **As you improve your FICO® scores, you'll pay less for credit.**

   "APR, on a 30-year fixed-rate mortgage for a person with a FICO score between 760 and 850 is 3.15 percent. For a person with a credit score between 620 and 639, the national average APR is 4.74 percent. The difference in interest rates shows why it's so important to get your credit history on track before applying for a loan." *With my credit score, what interest rates? By Dr. Don Taylor, Ph.D., CFA, CFP, CASL Bankrate.com http://www.bankrate.com/finance/credit/credit-score-interest-rates.aspx*

   Thank you Congress, it's not often when the government gives things away. On December 1st, 2004, the Fair and Accurate Credit Transactions Act (FACTA) went into existence. What's the big deal about FACTA? All three major credit bureaus, (Trans Union, Equifax, and Experian) now supply consumers with a free credit report upon request once every 12 months. Prior to FACTA individuals would have to wait for a credit rejection letter in order to obtain a free report. Alternatively, they could pay a company to obtain their credit report.

The government has also favored us by enacting The Equal Credit Opportunity Act. The Equal Credit Opportunity Act prohibits creditors from discriminating against credit applicants on the basis of race, color, religion, national origin, sex, marital status, age, (provided the applicant has capacity to enter into a binding contract) because all or parts of the applicant income derives from any public assistance program or because the applicant has in good faith exercise any right under The Consumer Credit Protection Act.

Contact information for the three major credit bureaus:

Equifax:

P.O. Box 740241, Atlanta, GA 30374

800-685-1111 (questions regarding fraud 800-525-6285)

www.equifax.com

Experian: PO Box 2002, Allen, TX 75013

888-397-3742

www.experian.com

TransUnion: P.O. Box 2000, Chester, PA 19022

800-888-4213 (questions regarding fraud 800-680-7289)

www.transunion.com.

Acquire your annual credit report

1-877-322-8228

www.annualcreditreport.com

Identity Theft

Federal Trade Commission

1-877-IDtheft

www.consumer.gov/Idtheft

ALL ABOUT THE MONEY

Needs and wants! This is the best
summation of how people use their
credit. Makes no difference whether
it's a credit card or loan from a
financial institution; be it a credit
union, bank, or other types of lenders.
In a perfect world, the use of credit
would be solely based on needs and not
on wants. As a child, I learned about
credit from my grandmother at an early
age. If we couldn't afford it with
cash, we couldn't have it. The idea of
buying something on credit was almost
foreign. Not having cash meant saving
small amounts until you amassed enough
to purchase the service or good that
you needed. There were times she needed
to acquire a good or service which
necessitated the use of credit!
However, every effort was made to
relinquish the debt as soon as possible
so that credit did not become a burden
causing her sleepless nights and
constant worry about whether or not the
credit would be paid off in a

reasonable time.

What are needs? Needs are items you must have in order to survive. Food, shelter, water, clothing are the essential four items an individual requires for survival. In today's world, I would include transportation, whether public or private, and I would also include technology. It is almost a handicap not having a working knowledge of technology or Internet connectivity at your disposal. At no point did I say the filet mignon weekly for dinner, Evian, the 5000 square foot cape, Donna Karan apparel, or the Mercedes-Benz super warp speed Internet connectivity. Individuals will take basic needs and because of the desire for social acceptance inflate their cost, their reach, their aesthetic appeal in order to fulfill some type of societal pressure. It could be a societal value or it could be simply self-indulgence.

When individuals are no longer

acquiring basic needs for survival they
are chasing and acquiring wants. I want
this. I want that. Give me that. I'll
take that one. I want more of that and
I must update that. Once that moment
has passed, many of these individuals
are looking for the next item, service,
or good to satisfy a craving which will
ensure moments of happiness. These
moments have an expiration date: no one
knows exactly how long the moments will
last. Still, they do not last long
enough. My friend Andre Mannain, says
all the time, "If some is good more is
better." He wants more. Andre says
this regarding customers for his
signage business, the horse power in
his truck for hauling heavy work items,
and for towing his recreational items.
Do not have this philosophy "If some is
good more is better" for consumption of
goods and services with the use of
credit. It's obvious there is a glut
of overconsumption. Take note of the
amazing numbers of storage units which

have cropped up all across the country
to store the excess items Americans can
no longer fit in their homes.

**Signs of financial troubles related to
credit card:**

1. Credit cards are near full capacity
   (almost maxed out)
2. Multiple cards are near max limit
3. Failure to reduce credit card balances
4. Having trouble paying your bills on
   time (constantly incurring late fees)
5. You can only afford to make minimum
   payments.
6. Using credit cards to cover most, if
   not all, of your life expenses

**Credit approval is based on the three
C's of credit plus one**

1. **Character** - do you pay your bills when
   they come due?
2. **Capacity** - have you worked long enough
   in a position which can provide funds

for repayment based on the credit you may use in the future?

3. **Capital** - your ability to repay a loan. Do you have assets such as savings, investments, property, which could be used to repay debt if needed?

4. **Credit mix** - what kinds of credit usage do you currently have if any (car loan, home loan student loans, medical loans, and so on)?

Some of the factors that will be used over time to increase or decrease your credit score will be:

1. **Bill or loan payment history (whether bills are paid on time or late)**

2. **Length of credit history (how long have you used credit)**

3. **Constantly attempting to procure new forms of credit**

4. **How exposed is your credit usage (50%, 60%, 70%, 80%, 90% of overall credit has been used). A $10,000 credit card limit may likely have a $9,000 balance.**

5. **The various forms of credit you use (credit card car longs mortgage student loans…)**

Know this, ***"Sorry doesn't fix the lamp!"*** Once the lamp is broken you can put the pieces together with super crazy glue, but it will never look the same; it may work and even add a great story during a dinner party, but ***sorry the patched lamp will not recapture its*** original luster. Once your credit is broken, it will take lots and lots of work to get your score to where it was, and even more work to get it beyond that point.

Americans save very little of their post-tax income. Once the government state and local municipalities have taken what they believe is rightfully theirs from what you've rightfully earned, you are left what remains (your disposable income). Americans are great at paying debts to creditors but the one creditor they should pay before everyone else is themselves. That's right, pay yourself before you pay other people. Now that you've paid yourself first, "tell them what they've won! You've won the right to have money put away for a rainy day!" The essential ingredient of survival (victory) is preparation. Preparation in practice or training, prepares one for the unexpected and one must prepare for the unexpected, and when the unexpected appears you are ready because you expected it to happen.

My seventh grade math teacher, Mr. Thorn, would often say, "You don't plan to fail, you fail to plan." Mr. Thorn had all these little quotes that for some reason entered my head, found a place, and never left. Mr. Thorn also used to say, "SOP, standard operating procedures." I suppose in another life, Mr. Thorn would've been a general or benevolent dictator. I learned a lot from Mr. Thorn. I plan for the unexpected, develop good habits and allow those good habits to be routine. Thanks, Mr. Thorn!

There are copious reasons why we lack capacity to save. We want what we want when we want it. We are bombarded by a myriad of advertisements telling us what's wrong with us.

- ✓ **your car is too old**
- ✓ **you're too fat**
- ✓ **you're not smart, you're not cool**
- ✓ **your sexual parts do not work**
- ✓ **you need to be at this particular location on your pending vacation**
- ✓ **your teeth are not white enough**
- ✓ **your teeth are not straight enough**
- ✓ **you're not happy enough**
- ✓ **you're too happy**
- ✓ **you smoke too much**
- ✓ **you drink too much**
- ✓ **You don't drink enough**
- ✓ **you don't smoke enough**
- ✓ **you don't blank this item**

ALL ABOUT THE MONEY

✓ **You don't blank that thing**

How do you fix what they tell you
you need to fix? How do you acquire
what they tell you that you need to
acquire? How do you go where they tell
you you need to go? How do you remedy
whatever it is that needs to be
remedied? Like the cavalry going into
battle you do what seems to be
absolutely completely natural, and
somewhat organic: you charge and you
charge and you charge! You're not
alone. Many of us are guilty as
charged (pun intended).

Grandma used to say, "Prevention
is better than cure!" My grandmother,
Myrtle, a small woman scantly above
5'2" tall, hundred fifteen pounds (of
pure energy), with the lack of
secondary education, was one of the
wisest persons I've ever met in my
life. Her sage advice encompassed all
parameters of life. Her advice is

timely, well thought-out, and clearly provided guidance which paved the way for ultimate success. Prevention is better than cure was used as a precursor to decisions large and small for all occasions. She said, "It is better to avoid a mistake, it is better to not get into something that will be extremely difficult to get out." So before I made purchases, I often heard those words echo in my head. Before you buy the luxury car, the mini mansion, the expensive golf clubs think about the cost down the road. Can you truly afford these items or services for which you are drawn to? Would it serve you better to walk away from the purchase, return home, and think about it? If after a good a night sleep and some deliberation you've decided this good or service is something you require, and will not hamper your financial well-being down the road, then by all means acquire it.

ALL ABOUT THE MONEY

Financial issues are not just financial problems. They can affect your state of mind, your relationships, stress levels and can lead to mental or physical manifestations being displayed, causing you great pain.

Marketers, psychologist and retailers work in concert to develop effective means of selling you products or services you may not need. Things always look better in the store, showroom and sound much more appealing when it's being pitched by a salesperson in their controlled environment. The lighting is immaculate and made to emphasize the high points of the product. The sales pitch being delivered is generated from a proven script and is much more effective when you're in the moment. You may need to walk away and escape the moment, returning only when you have used time to ponder your pending desire. Grab a pen, grab a piece paper, have a seat.

Create a list of pros and cons. It may seem hackneyed but it is effective for most decisions one is contemplating on moving towards. At the end of the day, this may not be your ideal method of decision-making. However, do not rush into major financial decisions. The ramifications may be unseen but the devastation may be felt for years to come.

Insurance

There are some people for whom once they leave, the connection is broken and the effort to regain the connection is seldom rekindled. Then there are those from whom you receive a call and instant time warp commences. Prior to the weekend of July 4, 2014, I received a call from a friend I had not seen in years. Mike Pellazarri was one of those guys I grew up with, lost contact, regained contact, and at some point the cycle would repeat itself. We walked home from school together instead of taking the bus. We hung out and always shared laughs. "Hey what's up? How you been? Great! And you? blah blah blah and some more blah blah blah and we ended with blah blah blah, come to the cookout on Saturday man, can't wait to see you..." People move from place to place, lose contact, and regain contact. That's just how our lives are these days. You are back to where you were as if you never left, and the friendship that once existed returns to its original strength as strong and as jubilant as it ever.

A cookout became a quasi high school reunion. I saw Mike, Chris, Tom, Little Mike, Mason, a few of the females we went to school with and a list of others with relevant faces but hidden names. We talked about family life, what we had done, what we were up to, and who was in contact with whom. When we came across Carmine's name I was shocked to learn someone I grew up with had passed away a few years ago, right around 40 years of age, from a heart attack. I was saddened as well as shocked. He was a jovial guy, good for a laugh and good for a talk. Had I known of his passing I would've paid my respects. I'm not sure if Carmine was married, divorced, separated or had children. My mind flashed from Carmine to concern about his family's emotional well-being in addition to their financial state.

Insurance, it's something most of us delay even though the inevitable omnipresent conclusion to our birth is our death. No one knows how we die or when we die, but we die. You can't take any of your worldly possessions with you (well if you're a Pharaoh you're the exception to the rule). The rest of us cannot take our loved ones when we go, nor would we want to shorten someone's life to please our selfish desires for eternal companionship. Here's what you can do for those who remain once you are gone; ensure that their day-to-day existence without you will be as pleasant as possible. My friends, this can be accomplished most easily with one product and that product is life insurance. The amount you require will be up to you based on comfort level, age, health, lifestyle and needs. The form of insurance you buy will best be decided when you speak with someone in the profession.

The two dominant forms of life insurance are Whole Life and Term Life. Whole Life Insurance is defined by its name, its insurance you pay for your whole life. Whole life has savings wrapped into it which may make it more attractive for some people. Term insurance lives up to its name. You pay for a certain term: ten years, twenty years or thirty years and the term ends. There is no savings with term insurance.

Insurance buyers will have lower premiums (monthly or annual payments) the younger you purchase it. Insurance companies calculate life expectancies based on empirical data and the data says all things being equal insurance companies will have far more money come to them than they pay to policy holders at a future date. Insurance companies are not in the business of losing money.

Which one is right for you? It depends on many factors, but let's put it this way: term cost less and gives you greater financial coverage (protection dollar for dollar). Whole Life insurance can cost you five times more than Term insurance for identical dollar value amounts. A thirty-year-old man would pay $18 per month for $50,000 in coverage with Term insurance. This same thirty-year-old man would pay $90.00 per month (or more) if he purchased a Whole Life Insurance Policy. Considering this fact he may be able to acquire an insurance policy of $100,000, $200,000, or $300,000, of pure insurance coverage. If the unthinkable were to happen, this man's family may have an easier time with post-death costs which will exist and require financial navigation.

The downside when the term (period) ends there is no more insurance coverage. There is also the cost of getting reinsured. Twenty years after the term expires you are twenty years older which means your rates will be higher at renewal. Whole life's premiums will remain intact for your whole life.

"But there's a savings plan with whole life!" Sure, absolutely and that's a good thing. Yet we all have car insurance, which covers our car, or homeowners' insurance which covers our home, or our renters' insurance which just covers our apartment. Insurance company inside information: It may take two years to accumulate cash value and years for you to have substantial cash build up. Point is, if you are going to use Whole Life as an investment, there may be a better way.

Here's more dirt: if you borrow your own money from your life insurance policy you will be charged interest. One more nugget of information, funds withdrawn and not repaid will lessen the payout to beneficiaries upon the insured's passing (if you're insured for $100,000 policy and *"borrow"* $20,000 upon death, beneficiaries will receive $80,000 ($100,000 - $20,000 = $80,000). The insurance company has deducted $20,000 based the amount borrowed.

The following is an example of term coverage based on age, length of coverage and dollar amount.

$500,000 Term Coverage

Age	10 Years	20 Years	30 Years
30	$14.00	$20.00	$33.00
35	$14.00	$21.00	$37.00
40	$ 17.00	$28.00	$47.00
45	$27.00	$43.00	$74.00
50	$ 38.00	$ 60.00	$99.00
55	$56.00	$96.00	$312.00
60	$83.00	$156.00	$745.00
65	$135.00	$296.00	$945.00
70	$211.00	$487.00	$1,225.00

Dollar amounts may vary based on gender, health, age, occupation, geographic location and a few other factors.

Insure your children. This may appear to be a lugubrious thought; however hear me out. Two reasons why you should insure your child:

1. In addition to the emotional toll of losing a child there is a clear and

present financial cost which will not be discounted because a child has died.

2. Children covered under an insurance policy will be given a status of guaranteed insurability. A child diagnosed with an illness may eliminate their future insurability (deem them uninsurable as an adult). However, if they are insured as children they won't be uninsurable as adults. The insurance company will cover them as adults (despite being diagnosed with an illness) because you covered them when they were younger (great parenting on your part). As an adult, they can purchase as much as five times the coverage amount they had as a child ($10,000 as a child, $50,000 as an adult). Life insurance has the unique super power of mutation. Life insurance can change its form to fit your needs. The following are a few of the forms life insurance will exhibit:

Whole Life Insurance

1. Lifetime protection

2. Level premium (payments)
3. Cash value
4. Live to 100 policy pays you insured amount

Term Life Insurance

1. Protection (Nothing else)
2. Starts and ends at a specific duration
3. Cash value does not exists
4. Level premium (payments)

Other forms of Life Insurance

✓ Variable Life
✓ Universal Life
✓ Joint Life
✓ Limited Pay
✓ Joint and Survivor Life
✓ Accident and Disability
✓ Long-Term Care
✓ Single Pay

Last take on insurance companies. Insurance companies may guarantee you 3%-6% rate of return on your money.

Sounds tempting since its guaranteed, but insurance companies know that the financial markets have generated better than 9% over the last 30 years. Through good times and bad, that's the average return for the financial markets. Who keeps the extra percentage points? Who still pays fees for management of your money? You do. I'm sure you don't mind that, or do you?

Investing

"How many millionaires do you know who have become wealthy by investing in savings accounts? I rest my case."

Robert G. Allen

"An investment in knowledge always pays the best interest." *Benjamin Franklin*

Benjamin Franklin's statement was profound in his day and has even greater prominence today. I cannot foresee a time where this statement would lack merit or be deemed passé.

In the summer of 2014 elected officials of New York State were debating wisely a proposal to mandate CPR as a graduation requirement. Logic would say it's absolutely a fantastic move which could save dozens of lives for years to come. These same elected officials who proposed CPR as a mandate for graduation have completely omitted the thought of **Financial CPR.** Mandated, graduation required **Financial CPR,** could save hundreds of thousands of individuals (if not millions) from possible future financial dilemmas.

The United States Bureau of Labor Statistics accumulated a very interesting set of statistics. When I first read the data I was shocked; however, I endeavored to do all that I could to realize a position on this data chart, which would not cost me great consternation regarding my financial situation. The following information may expedite your urgency to be better with money, investing, and spending than you ever have in your entire life.

Out of 100 people whose goal at age 25, was to have a fortune at age 65:

- ✓ 1 was wealthy. They made it
- ✓ 4 had enough income to retire
- ✓ 3 were working because they had to
- ✓ 29 were deceased
- ✓ 63 were dependent on family, friends, or welfare

I carry these statistics on a card laminated in my wallet. What portion of these statistics will represent you when you decide to retire?

"The world is watching how we walk and how we talk. We must have the highest standards of morality, ethics and integrity if we are to continue to have influence." Billy Graham

Prior to the most recent financial

collapse in the early stages of the
2000 decade, many individuals sought
out financial advisors. Financial
advisors were given the all-
encompassing task of providing
financial advice and support to clients
enabling them to make sound financial
decisions.

As the financial industry recovers
post-crisis and the global regulatory
community takes a stiffer approach in
strengthening rules, much more is
expected of financial institutions in
the area of financial management.
Corporate collapses such as Enron and
WorldCom have ushered in a wave of firm
backlash at corporate America. Full
and complete financial disclosure,
corporate governance and ethical
responsibility have become the
watchwords of the global financial
industry. The battle will forever be
waged to regain and maintain the trusts
of stakeholders, shareholders,
customers and the general public at

large. Corporations may find it costly and perhaps end their existence if they should deviate from the highest ethical standards in their day to day operations and corporate policy.

Selfishness! Selfishness with a little greed sprinkled in plus huge payouts and you can see a tangible formula for problems. Well it's the average person's time to be selfish. I know mom, dad, grandma, nan-nah mo, Uncle Tony, Father Danny, Pastor Will, Rabbi Mark all said selfishness and greed are bad. Stay focused on what you want financially, educate yourself, periodically check your accounts, and ask questions (why, how and when). Michael Douglas said, when he played Gordon Gekko in the movie Wall Street, "Greed is good!" I surmise if individuals took a selfish greed stance when it came to monitoring the growth of their individual accounts this would have kept financial managers and

financial institutions on alert. As my
late Aunt Violet once said to me on a
few occasions, "Be careful who you
trust."

The onset of financial planning
starts with setting financial
objectives. The plan (objectives) are
personal and vary according to
investor's tastes and preferences such
as: investment horizons, annual income,
assets, debts, risk tolerance, net
worth, health, family size, and place
most likely to live when working days
are done. Once this is decided, how
will assets be directed to attain an
investor's goals? Asset allocation is
an investment strategy used to balance
risk enabling returns to march toward
the stated financial objectives over a
given period of time.

Possible asset allocation for an individual
diversifying investment with a plan to
minimize capital (financial) risk:

- ✓ 20% international blue chip stocks
- ✓ 20% domestic blue chip stocks
- ✓ 15% midcap stocks
- ✓ 10% small cap stocks
- ✓ 10% cash reserves
- ✓ 5% real estate
- ✓ 10% gold and silver
- ✓ 10% corporate and municipal bonds

ALL ABOUT THE MONEY

Social Security should not be your retirement plan. Social Security should be a supplement to your living expenses. The government has changed the administration of Social Security benefits to help extend the life of the benefit. Most individuals will not collect until age 70. The government has figured that a few of us who do not take great care of our health may not make it to the age of collection or live beyond that age. Morbid but true. This means fewer individuals who will be collecting government benefits. The second item which will have a major impact is changing the average working years' calculation. The old method used the 10 highest years of earnings. (Fantastic because generally you will have your best earning years near retirement) the new calculation uses the average of your highest 35 years of earnings. Spreading the earnings over 35 years and averaging it will drastically reduce the amount an individual will collect at age 70. Become a progressive investor. Sure you have no clue how long you will live; therefore, take steps to have additional income during the years when you can no longer work fulltime to support your living expenses.

Investment strategies (asset allocation) can and should be adjusted when it is rational and prudent. The overall objective should enable a person to generate a steady combination of growth, income, and capital preservation.

Investment Strategies

Preservation of Capital This strategy is designed for individuals who may need access to their funds in a short period of time (10-15 years). Clients may tend to be worrisome as they endeavor to increase assets but their concerns of loss dominate investment options. Safeguarding capital is the most important feature of this particular strategy of investing with the least possible risk.

Balance This strategy outlines mixes a portfolio as evenly as possible. 50% of a client's funds will be allocated to midcap stocks and 50% will be allocated to corporate and or municipal bonds. Fifty-fifty is not the only option. A client can allocate 25% real estate, 25% blue chip stocks, 25% international blue chip stocks, 25% pressure metals (gold, silver, platinum), or whatever mix they choose as being right for them.

Growth This strategy is designed for individuals with a long term-plan. Their objective is mainly focused on growth of the principal investment. This objective requires an investment portfolio proficiently managed and monitored. As time goes by, observations of performance and measurement expectations being met (or not being met) may necessitate slight adjustments.

Income This strategy outlines a plan for investing in capital growth but also provides a source of income (in the short-term or years down the road). Income may be in the form of real estate investments or dividends from stocks, or perhaps recouping the investments from state, federal, or local bonds.

Insurance policy Clients should include a life insurance policy that would cover the balances of any outstanding debt. Life insurance can and should be implemented as a tax-free way to transfer family wealth to the next generation.

Savings and Investment Grid					
Type of Investment	Degree of Risk	Yield	Maturity Time	Ease of Acquiring Cash	Investment Amount Required
Bank Acct	Extremely Low	Fixed at low to extremely low rate	N/A -*not applicable*	Super Easy	Generally $1 or more
CD	Extremely Low	Fixed at low to extremely low rate	Varies 3 months to 2 years	Somewhat restricted based on time locked into CD	Generally $500 or more
Money Market	Very Low	Low to modest rate	N/A -*not applicable*	Very Easy	Generally $500 or more
Gov't Bonds	Low to Modest	Low to modest rate	3 months to 30 years	Restricted to some degree until maturity	Generally $25 or more, or as much as $10,000 (T-bill)

Savings and Investment Grid					
Type of Investment	Degree of Risk	Yield	Maturity Time	Ease of Acquiring Cash	Investment Amount Required
Corporate Bonds	Modest	Modest to high	Up to 30 years	Varies	Generally $100 or more
Mutual Funds	Modest to Elevated	Varies, modest to elevated rates of return (potentially high)	N/A - not applicable	Not very difficult	Generally $25-$50 minimum per month or you can invest a greater amount in a lump sum or periodically
ETF'S Exchange Traded Funds	Low to Modest	Varies, modest to elevated rates of return (potentially high)	N/A - not applicable	Not very difficult	Price based on open market activities
Common Stock	Modest to Elevated	Varies, modest to elevated rates of return (potentially high)	N/A - not applicable	Not very difficult	Price based on open market activities

Investment Ladder of Risk
HIGH RISK   Futures
Medium Risk   Stocks   Mutual Funds   Corporate Bonds   Exchange Traded Funds
Low Risk   Savings Account   Money Market Funds   Certificate of Deposits   Government Securities   Treasury Bills, Notes & Bonds

"Invest your money in CD's."
That's what my dad said and his dad
said. CD's are safe! There is truth
in that statement. Tony invests $1,000
into a CD (Certificate of Deposit) at
his bank. He agrees to leave the money
with his bank for two years. Tony will
receive a very low rate of interest
(around 1%) and his money is locked in
for that period of time. If an
emergency occurs and Tony needs a
portion of his money or all his money
he can have it but for a fee
established by the bank. Tony has made
the choice between safety and growth.

Has someone close to you
emphasized financial growth and safety
by proclaiming, "CD's are safe!" Ask
your father about the **Rule of 72**. What
is the **Rule of 72**? Well a very long
time ago, some crazy mathematician
figured out that **72 divided** by the

interest rate will show you roughly how many years it takes for your money to double. Conversely if you need to know the number of years your money would double based on a particular interest rate *divide 72* by the number of years and you will arrive at the interest rate needed to double your money. Please remember this is not an exact calculation of years or interest rates but it is a good starting point.

The Formula for finding the interest rate needed to double savings 72 ÷ number of years = interest rate		
72 ÷	The number of years funds are invested	**The interest rate required to double your savings**
72 ÷	2	**= 36.00%**
72 ÷	4	**= 18.00%**
72 ÷	5	**= 14.40%**
72 ÷	6	**= 12.00%**

The Formula for finding the number of years needed to double savings 72 ÷ interest rate = number of years		
72 ÷	**Interest rate**	**Number of years it will take for your savings to double**
72 ÷	3% rate of a generous CD	= 24 *It will take twenty-four years for your savings to double*
72 ÷	9%	= 8 *It will take eight years for your savings to double*
72 ÷	12% the stock markets average rate of return for the past three decades	= 6 *It will take six years for your savings to double*
72 ÷	19.99% average credit card interest rate	= 3.6 *It will take almost four years for your savings to double*

The sooner you begin investing, the greater the impact (growth of funds) down the road. The age you begin saving is monumental to the amount you will accrue at the age you decide to take the savings and use them to live life as you dreamed. I can recall when my grandma Myrtle was teaching me how to cook. She always stressed patience.

"Son, there is no need to turn the fire up to extra, extra high heat. If you do this food will burn and lack true mouthwatering flavor. You need to plan your meal. Get your seasonings. Get your pots and pans. Get your ingredients: fish or chicken, rice and vegetables. Get your olive oil. Turn on the fire and put the pan or pots on the fire. Allow your pots and pans to warm. Gently place your ingredients one after the other into your pots and pans. Allow the ingredients to cook slowly; allow them to simmer. Just before your meal is done the aroma will fill the air. Go set your table, pour out your drinks. Call your family, your friends, dinner guests to the table. Ask everyone to sit and say a prayer thanking the Lord. Finally, serve your meal."

Her point was well taken. If I waited to the last minute, I would rush into the kitchen, blast the heat up to extra, extra high, cooking the food quickly and unevenly or perhaps burning the food. All those invited to dine will surely be disappointed in what is clearly an imitation of something palatable. If I planned and started the meal at a reasonable time, I may have a few issues but certainly I would avoid a major culinary fiasco.

You cannot treat guests to meals which are below the quality of fast food franchise. Do not your treat investments like fast food; as if it were an afterthought because you chose not to prepare a home cooked meal. The

following chart will demonstrate how
starting early pays off in the long
run. Please note, the higher the rate
of return, the greater the amount
one accumulates.

The following is a chart showing the possible outcomes of investments based on the age investing begins.						
Age	Amount saved per month	Number of years to retire	4% rate of return over savings period	7% rate of return over savings period	9% rate of return over savings period	12% rate of return over savings period
25	$50	35	$59,000	$132,000	$235,000	$594,000
25	$100	35	$118,000	$264,000	$471,000	$1,100,000
25	$250	35	296,000	660,000	1,179,000	2,970,000
30	$50	30	$45,000	$90,000	$148,000	$324,000
30	$100	30	$91,000	$181,000	$296,000	$649,000
30	$250	30	$229,000	$452,000	$740,000	$1,632,000

The following is a chart showing the possible outcomes of investments based on the age investing begins.						
Age	Amount saved per month	Number of years to retire	4% rate of return over savings period	7% rate of return over savings period	9% rate of return over savings period	12% rate of return over savings period
35	$50	25	$34,000	$61,000	$92,000	$176,000
35	$100	25	$69,000	$122,000	$184,000	$352,000
35	$250	25	$174,000	$306,772	$461,000	$888,000
40	$50	20	$25,000	$40,000	$56,000	$94,000
40	$100	20	$51,000	$81,000	$112,000	$189,000
40	$250	20	$128,000	$203,772	$282,000	$474,000

ALL ABOUT THE MONEY

The previous (savings and investing
grid above) chart demonstrates the
minimum cost to open some mutual funds.
However, these funds can be used for
other investments as well. Later we
will discuss ETF's (Exchange Traded
Funds), stocks, and bonds. The
fundamental purpose of the chart above
was to demonstrate how little an
individual actually has to save per
month in order to achieve some
financial assurance 20 years, 25 years,
30 years, 35 years down the road. Think
of it this way: $50 a month equates to
a $1.67 per day.

✓ How much does a cup of coffee cost?
✓ How much does a hamburger cost?
✓ How much does a can of soda cost?
✓ How much does your favorite junk food
snack cost?

I'm willing to venture it is more
than the cost of investing a $1.67 per
day. Placing your investment dollars in
these terms may make it easier for an

individual to allocate these resources to some type of investment. Breaking down the daily investment required did not increase its palatability. Well then, let's simply cut the total in half that's right $25. Reducing the amount to $25 per month, the breakdown per day is simply $0.83.

✓ Is that less than your typical giant burger?
✓ Is that less than fast food mega meal?
✓ Is that less than a can of soda?
✓ Is that less than a cup of coffee?
✓ Is that less than dollar menu french fries?
✓ Is that less than a lottery ticket?

I would venture to guess $0.83 is an easier reach for most individuals reading this. Yes, the end payout will be less but there will be an end payout.

Through prudent investing you've

earned quite a bit of money. Now what?
Well the growth of money is one stage
and the proper allocation of it for the
remainder of your life is the second
stage. There are two things a person
should never outlive: their children
and their money. You cannot watch your
children twenty-four seven but these
days you can watch your money twenty-
four seven. Be observant of the money
invested on your behalf.

The following chart will demonstrate how withdrawals may last with prudent use.		
Savings Accumulated at Retirement	Monthly withdrawals based on accumulated dollar will provide a life expectancy of 10 years for the accumulated funds	Monthly withdrawals based on accumulated dollar amount will provide a life expectancy of 20 years for the accumulated funds
$250,000	$2,744	$1,769
$300,000	$3,293	$2,123
$400,000	$4,391	$2,831
$500,000	$5,489	$3,538
$1,000,000	$10,978	$7,077
$1,500,000	$16,467	$10,615
$2,000,000	$21,955	$14,153
$3,000,000	$32,933	$21,230
If fewer funds are withdrawn per month the expected financial life of the invested funds are extended.		

"You're short on ears and long on mouth." John Wayne

This quote fits those who would proselytize how fortunate buyers of their stock pick will be. Their knowledge is so far above all others; it's a "can't miss opportunity." Investigate! Prior to running out to call your stocker broker, or going online to press the buy button via your online trading account because of a recommendation from a friend or family member, investigate! Do your due diligence and research the stock yourself. Many people have a stock tip or hot-stock recommendation based purely on hearsay or self-interest.

✓ **Invest in what you know**
✓ **Invest in what interests you**
✓ **Invest in what gives you pleasure**
✓ **Invest in the products your friends are buzzing about**

- ✓ Invest in what grandma and her friends are laughing about
- ✓ Invest in what the cool kids are buying (a prerequisite for being cool is spending money on cool stuff). It's a short term investment but it could be profitable
- ✓ Invest in what everyone is eating
- ✓ Invest in the place where everyone eats or drinks

A solid base of operation from which to advance your investment tools is the best plan.

Warning: avoid news outlets and various forms of social media for your stock advice. I'm sure the posting on Facebook, or the tweet you re-tweeted is 100% true! Is it really true? News outlets and social media never sleep. Content is needed to fill a 24-7 thirst for new information. People posting at 3 a.m. because of loneliness, insomnia, or sinister reasons may not provide the best tips. I urge you to be diligent

before you act and move with intelligence concerning your financial dealings.

Do not fear the stock market. I know you've heard of or experienced crashes, Black Mondays, other black-days, and crash-crash! The stock market is scary! It is scary consistent. The market has returned 9% over the past 30 years. This encompasses crashes, black-days, ups, downs, global economic strife and political strife which have come and gone and will return. The stifling fear which lingers about hindering individuals preventing them from investing is the risk loss. Fortune favors those who embrace fear. If you sit on the sidelines with fear then you are correct you will not lose a thing. Or will you? You will definitely watch others fail, but with unassailable truth you will watch many others succeed. The unmitigated gall of success relishes its ability to overlook you and find others willing to walk with risk. My friends we should all endeavor to embrace some risk! Stocks! Stocks may be your opening financial entre into the world of investing. Here is a look at how and why people may invest capital into stocks.

What are stocks? Stocks are investment vehicles which provide the purchaser with a percentage of ownership in a particular company. Stocks are sold in shares. An individual can purchase 1 share, 1,000 shares, 10,000 shares (limits of purchase amounts allowed may vary from company to company). The total amount of stocks a company has issued in the market divided by what an investor owns, will determine the percentage of ownership an individual investor has in the company. Let's say Violet buys 1,000 shares of stock from ABC Cars and ABC Cars has 100,000 shares outstanding. Violet's percentage of ownership is 1%.

Shares purchase ÷ Shares outstanding = Percent owned

1,000 ÷ 100,000 = .01

Convert to a percentage

.01 x 100 = 1%

Stocks may also provide an additional source of income (as one gets older) in the form of a dividend. Dividends will be paid to the owner of the stock for each share that individual owns. Assume Violet's stocks in ABC Cars will pay $2.00 per share for each share of stock owned by an investor. Violet owns 1,000 shares of ABC Cars. Violet will be sent a check for the amount of $2,000.

Violet's shares of ABC Cars x Dividend = Dividend Paid Out

1,000 x $2.00 = $2,000

Companies do not always have a dividend. Some companies will issue more stock which is called a split. ABC Cars announces a split of two to one. Violet owns 1,000 shares of ABC Cars; Violet will get an additional share for every share she owns. Violet will now own 2,000 shares of ABC Cars stock. ABC Cars will give Violet an additional 1,000 shares of stock increasing her total amount to 2,000 shares.

Violet's shares of ABC Cars x split = New Stock Ownership Amount (2 to 1)

1,000 x 2 = 2,000 (2,000 new amount post stock split)

Stocks may also appreciate over time. Appreciation does not involve money, it means over time the value of a company's stock may increase. Violet purchases ABC Cars stock at a price of $10 per share, 10 years ago. However, ABC Cars has done so well selling cars. The value of their stock has now increased to $73 per share. If Violet sold her shares of ABC Cars stock, she would make $63 per share. The $63 would be the difference between what she purchased it for and what she can now sell it for.

ABC Cars stock has appreciated quite a bit since Violet purchased the stock, 10 years ago. Stock prices may also fall because of economic functions or poor management. Violet purchases ABC Cars stock at a price of $10 per share 10 years ago. However, ABC Cars has done so poorly selling cars. The value of their stock has now decreased to $3 per share. If Violet sold her sock she would lose $7 per share. The $7 would be the difference between what she purchased it for and what she can now sell it for.

Investors may purchase stock in another form called preferred stock. What's the difference? Common stockholders have a say (vote)

regarding board of directors and other
company issues which may occur.
Preferred stockholders do not have a
say (vote). Common stock holders over
time may not receive the same
generosity with dividend payouts as
preferred stock holders. The upside of
preferred stock is that it's viewed
similarly to a bond and in the event of
company financial problems
(bankruptcy), preferred stock owners
would be paid before common stock
owners. In essence, common stock is
ownership of a company preferred stock
is a loan to a company. All stocks
have an added cost of commissions
(money in the transactions related to
stocks). Commissions will be paid when
buying a stock and commissions will be
paid when the stock is sold.
Commissions may be discounted based on
the quantity of stock purchased from a
traditional or online broker.

The long-aged Mesopotamian idea of

buying a stock at a low price and selling it at a high price does not work for you. You can do the inverse: sell high and buy low. This is called shorting a stock. Shorting benefits investors when the market goes the other way (down). On average, the market falls three times faster than it rises. Intuitional investors know this and I am willing to venture they do this more than they let on.

My niece, Ana, read the previous paragraph and asked, "Please explain this **call put thing?**" Well Ana, ABC Cars stock is selling at a price of $19 per share: However, Violet feels that report in the media of mechanical advancement will affect the stock price in a positive manner. Just as Violet believes ABC Cars stock will rise and Tamara believes it will decline. Violet and Tamara would like to own 100 shares of ABC Cars stock. The cost to acquire 100 shares of ABC Cars stock is $1,900. They do not have the necessary funds to complete the transaction. Violet and Tamara can purchase option contracts. Each contract contains a batch of 100 shares of ABC Cars stock. They will enter the stock market as buyer and seller (polar opposites regarding how well or how poorly ABC Cars stock performs in the market). Violet purchases a **Call Option** for $0.75/share; she essentially invests $75 to control $1,900 worth of stock. Violet is buying one option contract of ABC Cars stock (she buys a **Call Option** believing it will increase in value). Since Violet has a **Call Option** with ABC Cars stock, she watches the stock market hunch play true and ABC Cars stock increase to $24 per share. Violet wins! Violet essentially will earn a profit of $5 per share (minus any fees and expenses). Tamara assumed ABC Cars stock would fall below $19 per share. Tamara purchased one contract of ABC Cars stock with a **Put** (she bought a **Put Option** believing ABC Cars stock would decrease in value despite the positive media reports). Violet's **Call Option** has gained value and Tamara's **Put Option** has lost value.

The inverse would be mildly calamitous for Violet (if the price of ABC Cars stock decreased) Violet would lose her $75. If ABC Cars stock fell to $14 per share Tamara would benefit. Tamara's instincts would have correctly played out ABC Cars stock falling from $19 to $14 per share. Tamara essentially would earn a profit of $5 per share (minus any fees and expenses). When someone shorts (believing a fall in the price of stock is imminent), they have unlimited risk because the stock can increase exponentially. Individuals who short stocks (believing a fall in the price of stock is imminent) must be absolutely comfortable with huge risk undertakings. Options also have an added risk of time. Contracts will expire on a certain date rendering them worthless. **At the very least the Call option buyer and the Put option will lose the $75 investment if the bottom falls out.**

Please note individuals acquiring options have control of stocks and individuals buying stocks have ownership of stocks.

I gave Ana an additional example:

When an investor buys a stock they are afforded ownership. Option buyers of Calls and Puts are not given the same treatment. Option buyers purchase an option contract (a Call **Option** or a **Put Option**). This provides the investor (option buyer) the choice to buy the stock at a specific specified price but the investor is not obliged to do so.

For example:

Ana is bullish; she believes XYZ Foods stock will increase in price, but she doesn't have $1,900 to buy a 100 shares XYZ Foods stock. The stock is currently selling for $19 per share. Ana expects the rise in price to be significant because of her research and news from various media outlets are positive. Buying a Call Option would give Ana control of 100 shares of XYZ Foods stock. Ana can purchase a Call option $1.32/per share. Let's say the stock does as Ana expects and rises to $25.50. Ana will reap $6.50 per share profit (minus fees and expenses). Ana did not spend $1,900 but she still gets to pocket $650.00 (minus fees and expenses). The fact is Ana used $132 to control 100 shares of stock.

Ana purchased a call option. Well why would she want to invest in this manner? There are many reasons. First, let's focus on the main one – money! An investor can buy a call option for quite a bit less cash than buying a stock outright. The call option will cost Ana $132 ($1.32 X

100). The "Ana example" demonstrates how she purchased a call option for $1.32 per share. She invested $132 ($1.32 X 100) controlling $1,900 worth of stock. The second reason is if the stock loses value despite all of Ana's insight she will only lose the invested $132 invested.

Stock		Bid	Ask	B/A Size	Hi	Lo	Vol.
ABC	$19.00	$1.29	$1.32	100x200	--	--	50,000

Buy to Open 1 contract of ABC July 17 2015 97.5 Call
Limit at $1.32
Estimated total $132.00*

A drawback of a Call Option is if the stock never rises above $19 or the bottom falls out the entire investment is lost. Options have an expiration date of 15, 30, 60, 90 days and so on. The closer the option gets to the expiration date the less time the option buyer has to make a profit.

If an investor felt the complete opposite outcome would happen regarding a stock they would buy a Put Option. The greater risk will often provide the greatest reward. There are times when investors should think of the Latin phrase **Sine Metu (without fear)** when investing. Find your **Sine Metu (without fear)** moment.

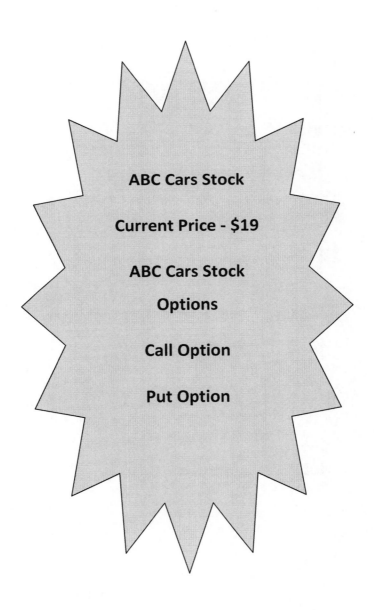

ABC Cars Stock

Current Price - $19

ABC Cars Stock

Options

Call Option

Put Option

Call Option Buyer – *Violet believes* **ABC Cars Stock** *will rise from $19 per share to $25 per share - Violet buys a* **Call option** *- The closer the stock gets to the price Violet expects the greater the profit.   If the stock falls below current price per share ($19 to $14 per share) losses can be devastating*

Put Option Buyer – Tamara

believes stock will fall from

$19 to $14 per share - The

closer the stock gets to the

price Violet expects the greater

the profit - If the stock rises

above the current price per

share ($19 to $25 per share)

losses can be devastating

If the risk of placing all your
hopes on a single investment keeps you
up at night, perhaps mutual funds are
for you? Well first off, it's not a
"mutual fun". Mutual fun is what
happens when you hang out with friends
and have a good time. A mutual fund is
an investment vehicle that is
professionally managed by a fund
manager. Their job is to allocate
resources in good times and bad, so
investors avoid huge losses and are in
a position to make gains in the market.

Are you still unsure what a mutual
fund is? Think of your socks for a
second. Imagine if you only had one
pair of socks to wear every day. If
something were to happen to your only
pair of socks, you'd be out of luck.
Now imagine you own ten pairs, twenty
pairs, thirty pairs, or more. If
something were to happen to one pair,
it's bad, but you have twenty-nine more

to choose from. Well, that's a mutual
fund. It's made up of several stocks
so if one stock has a bad day, it's
okay. Your mutual fund may also be
invested in bonds (with a cash reserve
to purchase other investment vehicles
as opportunities open up) and other
forms of investment options. Another
way to think about mutual funds is that
they're a basket full of stocks
sprinkled with other investments to
alleviate the stress of being all in on
one stock.

Mutual funds offer you an
additional bonus - fractional shares.
Let's say an individual has $60 and ABC
Cars stock costs $40 per share. A
buyer of ABC Cars stock will be able to
purchase only one share.   Once more,
we will use ABC Car. This time
applying it to mutual funds. ABC Cars
Mutual Fund costs $40 per share an
individual has $60; the individual can
purchase fractional shares. The buyer
of ABC Cars Mutual Fund will purchase

1.5 shares.

Cash on hand ÷ Cost of ABC Cars Mutual Fund = Number of shares

$60 ÷ $40 = 1.5

Three things I enjoyed most about helping clients when I worked as a financial representative:

1. Helping identifying goals
2. Setting a plan for success
3. The money I was paid

There is a downside which is sometimes ignored; the costs associated with the acquisition of mutual funds. Upfront cost on a mutual fund can be as large as five percent. Yes five percent. $100,000 invested will have $5,000 immediately divided amongst the financial advisor, their bosses and the company offering the mutual fund. Here's the kicker: there is an annual cost of up to 1.2% to manage the fund on a yearly basis. This may not appear to be a huge percent; however, based on the amount invested and the years under management, that's a ton of cash. Individuals can invest their money in two kinds of mutual funds; Load (Front-end load) and No-load (charges are delayed for a later time). A Load mutual fund is a fancy way to say, "sales charge." A No-load mutual fund is a fancy way to say, "fees being levied on investors at a later period of time."

The following are examples of mutual funds and their objectives. This list is not the entirety of mutual funds. Consult a financial representative to find information on other types of funds which may fit your investment goals.

✓ **Index Funds – these mutual funds duplicate the performance of an index like S&P 500.**

✓ **Equity Funds – these funds consists mostly of stocks. The aim here is** growth. A good option for the long-term investor.

✓ International Funds - these mutual funds only invest outside the United States.

✓ Social funds – these funds are for socially-conscious individuals. These funds are not invested in companies that sell or produce the following: alcohol, tobacco, weapons and so on.

The return on these funds may be lower than funds which do not discriminate based on company or industry.

✓ Target date funds – these funds were created to help individuals save for retirement. The target date may be for the year 2050. The fund starts out mostly with stocks (for growth) and switches to less risk financial instruments as the target date approaches.

✓ Income funds – these funds consist of bonds: government bonds and corporate bonds.

✓ Regional funds – these funds concentrate on companies in a particular region which may have greater growth than domestics companies. These funds may be invested in countries located in Europe, Asia, North America or Latin America.

✓ Sector funds – these funds are invested in a particular industry. These funds may focus on technology, health and so on.

✓ Money Market Funds – these funds are made up of short-term debt instruments. These funds are widely regarded as a safe place to put money. Think Government backed financial instruments (bonds, treasury bills).

Let's talk sin. We will not discuss the seven deadly sins:

✓ **<u>Pride</u>** / Vanity (Does not help if you are the Invisible Man)

✓ <u>Envy</u>

✓ <u>Gluttony</u>

✓ **Lust**

✓ **Anger** (Wrath)

✓ **Greed** (Covetousness)

✓ **Sloth** (Definitely my least favorite sin)

Despite these seven and grandma Myrtle's warnings of the dangers of sin, I say sin is good. Really! Yes it is! I find this fund interesting. For those individuals that are all in on bad things in life, this fund is for you. The Vice Fund (also known as Sin Fund) may be worth taking a look at.

"The fund has returned 23.84 percent over the past year, 17.40 percent over the past three years, and 19.42 percent over the past five years. As its name suggests, this fund invests in "sin" stocks, and its list of top holdings is littered with companies that conscientious investors love to hate, including Philip Morris,

ALL ABOUT THE MONEY

Lorillard, British American Tobacco, and Altria. Mixed in with these big names in tobacco are defense and weapons giants like Lockheed Martin and Raytheon, beer companies such as Carlsberg A/S and Molson Coors, and some gambling picks. The fund, which is a counterbalance to the socially responsible investing movement, seeks out sin names wherever it can find them, including in the United States, the United Kingdom, Belgium, and Hong Kong."

http://money.usnews.com/funds/mutual-funds/large-blend/vice-fund/vicex

Trailing Returns	
Year to date	4.2%
1 Year	23.8%
3 Years (Annualized)	17.4%
5 Years (Annualized)	19.4%
10 Years (Annualized)	9.7%

http://money.usnews.com/funds/mutual-funds/large-blend/vice-fund/vicex

Do not lose faith investing; there are more investment vehicles to grow your money. There is hope. Say hello to ETF's. What are ETF's? ETF's are Exchange-Traded Funds. An ETF is a security which tracks an index (S&P 500, New York Stock) or commodity (see chart below for a list of commodities). ETF's trade on an exchange just like

traditional stocks and can be bought
and sold as if they were stocks.
Mutual Funds will charge investors a
management fee as do ETF's; however,
investors will pay a fee that is
sizably less. Unlike stocks, ETF's
have a smaller expense ratio of 0.1% to
1%. One can see that over the life of
an investment, ETF's would return more
based on the smaller fees being
charged. ETF's will provide the
diversification of a mutual fund but
can be actively traded like stocks.
Investors can also use ETF's in the
time-tested strategy of buy-and-hold to
make profits over time.

Examples of Commodities			
Agriculture	Energy	**Industrial Metals**	Precious Metals
Frozen	Natural gas	*Steel*	Silver
Orange juice	Ethanol	*Lead*	Palladium
Soybean	Crude oil	*Aluminum*	Platinum
Lean Hog	Coal	*Copper*	Gold
Sugar	Heating oil	***Nickel***	

Still confused about ETF's? Think of it this way: the car or truck your grandfather Bill drove is comparable to a mutual fund. It's a quite large non-aerodynamic contraption with unimpressive gas mileage capabilities and not equipped with safety features (no Bluetooth, backup camera, blind spot detection, and a host of other modern features). Your grandfather

Bill's car continues to run, gets him
around, and serves a valuable purpose
as a mode of transportation. ETF's are
comparable to modern vehicles antilock
brakes, OnStar, backup camera, front
facing camera, hybrid, flex fuel
Bluetooth, keyless entry, push button
start, touchscreen, GPS, onboard
computer and a host of other items
which make today's vehicle far superior
to grandpa Bill's car.

Four major Index ETF's

Index	ETF Symbols
Nasdaq	QQQ
Dow	DIA
Russell 2,000	IWM
S&P 500	SPY

The last (but certainly not the
only remaining) investments that I will
focus on are bonds. A bond is a loan
given to a city, state, corporation or
federal government. Bonds are purchased
at a discount and redeemed face value
at a particular time in the future.
buys a $1,000 United States Government
Bond at a 50% discount. This means
Scott will pay $500 for the bond today
but at redemption (10 years, 20 years)
she will be paid $1,000. Bond
discounts may be less or greater based
on the type of bond and years to
majority (the date you can cash in the
bond to get your money). Bonds will
pose certain risk because they have an
inverse relationship with interest
rates. As interests increase, bonds
become more attractive and as interest
rates decline, bonds become less
attractive.

The following are some of the types of bonds that are available for purchase by investor:

- ✓ Treasury bonds matures 10 to 30 years pay interest twice per year issued in denominations of $1,000
- ✓ Savings bonds an example US government series EE bonds. Available in denominations of $50 to $10,000 purchase: at 50% of face value.
- ✓ Municipal bonds issued by local and state governments. Can also be issued by school districts
- ✓ Corporate bonds
- ✓ Convertible bonds (these bonds can be converted to stock within a limited period of time)

Diversify. Diversification is one of the key components when investing for your future. Think back to high school when you first saw that person that made your heart go "ah man," or

"yikes," or "damn" or "blank is so
hot!" Now imagine if you based all of
your hopes, dreams, happiness and
thoughts of; having a family, retiring,
holding hands on the beach at sunset,
scaling a mountain together and ski
trips solely on that one individual.
How disappointed would you be if at the
end of the day that individual did not
reciprocate your advances? You invested
so much time, effort, planning, perhaps
a little conniving to win their heart.
You could not even get a second of
their time. I can only venture to
guess you would be incontrovertibly
crushed! You did not diversify, you did
not look at other options. You did not
do your due diligence, asking
questions, reading, studying and
spreading your risk across a vast venue
of possibilities. Diversification is
simply using the options you have to
invest in your future. Putting it all
into one sector and hoping for the best
is just an unwise move.

Interested in knowing about interest? Interest has a direct effect on the outcome of the funds invested. Think about it this way. I like coffee. I drink coffee morning, noon and night doesn't matter. Why do I drink coffee morning, noon and night? Caffeine! Gets me jazzed up and I get things done! Think of interest as your financial caffeine because interests get things done. Coffee comes from all over the world. Coffee has many flavors and shades. You can get dark roast, light roast, medium roast and variations in between. Interest also has variations. There's simple interest, exact simple interest, compound interest - future value (the sum total value of an investment including principal added with the compound interest), and present value (an amount required to reach future amount of money based on a given rate of return).

ALL ABOUT THE MONEY

Simple interest the most basic form of interest to calculate: (To calculate simple interest multiplying the interest rate by the principal by the number of periods).

Interest = Principal X Rate X Time

$I = P \textbf{ X } R \textbf{ X } T$

Mr. Noel borrowed $1,000 for one year at a rate of 8%

$1,000 \textbf{ X } 8\% \textbf{ X } 1$

$80 is owed in interest. Therefore Mr. Noel will pay the lender, at the end of the term, $80 in interest plus the principal. The total repayment is $1,080.00.

What if the loan is for a period less than one year? What if the loan is for a period greater than one year? Here are two examples of how to figure out the interests being charged.

Mr. Noel borrowed $1,000 for 8 months at a rate of 8%

$I = P \textbf{ X } R \textbf{ X } T$

$1,000 **X** 8% **X** 8/12

Mr. Noel borrowed $1,000 for 30 months at a rate of 8%

I = P **X** R **X** T

$1,000 **X** 8% **X** 30/12

Compound interest

What is compound interest? Simply put, interest on your interest. Suppose two athletes are running a 100-yard dash. The first athlete is Andrew, a kid you grew up with, actually a pretty good athlete. He could definitely complete the 100-yard dash in respectable time. The second athlete is Usain Bolt, currently the fastest man in the world. Andrew is simple interest, Usain Bolt is compound interest. Who do you think is going to win?

Mr. Noel invests $1,000 for two years in an account that pays a rate of 8% compounded annually.

Formula I = P X R X T

$1,000	Original Principal
X 8%	Interest Rate
$80	Year one interest rate
+ $1,000	Year one Principal
$1080	Second year principal
X .8%	Interest Rate
$86.40	Year two interest rate
+ $1080	Second year principal
$1,166.40	Final compound amount
- $1,000	Original Principal
$166.40	Amount earned over two
	years via compound interests

Compound interest, along with time, are key components to reaching individual goals of financial security.

There is another way to invest called **Dollar Cost Averaging.** I'm going to imagine that most individuals do not have the ability to place $10,000, $20,000, $30,000 or more as a one-time investment. I will also venture to guess that most individuals may not be able to invest $500 here and $500 there. **Dollar Cost Averaging** can be the choice of individuals with limited funds. You have decided $70 per pay period is the amount which best suits your investment goals. If you are paid every two weeks, this would provide $140 per month for investing. If ABC Cars stock sells for $20 per share, $140 would provide you with 7 shares of ABC Cars stock month after month. ABC Cars stock increases to $30 per share your $140 will now purchase 4 shares of ABC Cars stock. The economy declines for a period of time. ABC Cars stock reflexes this with a decline in price to $5 per share, and now your $140 buys 28 shares of ABC Cars stock.

Over the life of investing, you will accumulate more stock when times are Spartan and you will accumulate less stock when times are thriving. **Dollar Cost Averaging** over a 10-year, 20-year, and 30-year period can provide you with a substantial amount of money for your retirement. There may be a time you and your financial advisor decide to exit ABC Cars stock and place in a less risky investment.

IRA's (Individual Retirement Account): another investment option

Congress created IRA's to help individuals save for retirement (often called a Traditional IRA).

IRA's can be invested in

✓ **Mutual Funds**

- ✓ Stocks
- ✓ Annuities
- ✓ Bonds
- ✓ U.S. Minted Coins

Traditional IRA's

- ✓ IRA's grow tax deferred (taxes are paid at future date)
- ✓ Taxes are paid at distribution (withdrawal)

Warning regarding Traditional IRA's: if you take an early distribution (withdrawing money before age 59 ½) the government will levy a 10% penalty on the taxable portion of the distribution (withdrawal), including any taxes which may be due. There are always exceptions to many of the financial rules and or penalties; the exceptions are:

- ✓ Excess medical bills
- ✓ First time homebuyer
- ✓ Death
- ✓ Disability

Nearly a decade after creating Traditional IRA's the government created the Roth IRA. Roth IRA's are not taxed by the federal government when distributions are taken (the investment was made with after tax dollars).

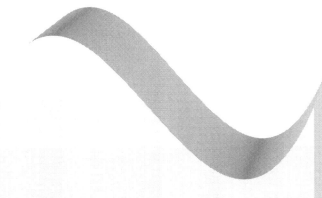

An individual who owns a Roth IRA can qualify for tax free distributions if

- ✓ Roth IRA owner is 59 ½ years old
- ✓ Roth IRA owner has become disabled
- ✓ Roth IRA has existed for a minimum of five years
- ✓ Roth IRA owner dies
- ✓ Roth IRA uses distribution as a first-time home buyer

ALL ABOUT THE MONEY

You cannot continuously place funds in an IRA. You must at some point take the money out. The United States Government wants to collect the taxes it's delayed collecting for decades. This mandatory government instituted required withdrawal is known as the **Required Minimum Distributions** or **RMD**. An individual must take RMD's no later than April 1 of the year they age into 70 ½. See your financial advisor or certified public accountant or professional tax preparer in order to figure out your RMD. Failure to take the proper RMD can result in a penalty of 50% on the amount that was not withdrawn.

Roth IRA's allow individuals to continue to add funds beyond age 70 ½. There are no RMD's required from individuals with Roth IRA's primarily because the government has already amassed tax revenue from this individual's earnings prior to the individual placing the money in the Roth IRA.

Traditional IRA's can be converted to Roth IRA's. See your professional tax preparer or financial advisor or certified public accountant to find out how this can be done.

Tell me lies,
Tell me sweet little lies
(Tell me lies, tell me, tell me lies)
Oh, no, no you can't disguise
(You can't disguise, no you can't
disguise)
Tell me lies
Tell me sweet little lies...

<u>Fleetwood Mac</u>

There is a major lie which needs to be dispelled. This lie can't be credited to **_The Boy Who Cried Wolf_** (but maybe it was his cousin). Let's call his cousin, **The boy who cried, "Your days will be cheaper when you retire** because you have fewer things to pay for." Well, **The boy who cried, "Your days will be cheaper when you retire because you have fewer things to pay for,"** has forsaken inflation. Inflation, dating back to 1925, has averaged about 3% per year and there are periods in history where inflation has actually surpassed the 3%. So you're capped out at $50,000 per year and retired. Well congratulations, but to cover your expenses over the 10 years you will need $67,000 per year and in 20 years you will need $90,000 per year. Yes, **The boy who cried, "Your days will be cheaper when you retire because you have fewer things to pay for,"** also forgot about taxes.

An individual with an investment worth $1 million will pay about $350,000. This amount may change in the future. The amount you saved, amassed, may not be the same amount you withdraw and spend. Let's say it's a Roth IRA instead of having $1 million.

You have $750,000 because you paid the tax upfront. As you get older your health may not be what it was when you were younger or perhaps based on genetics there are things waiting for you down the line. Medical expenses are huge for individuals as they get older. You still need to eat when you get older and the cost of food is not getting any cheaper. You will need to get around whether it's public transportation, private transportation or some type of taxi service. Those costs are all going to reflect an increase in fuel costs. If your health fails and you live in a nursing home or you require an aide to help you through your day-to-day living, those costs can be extremely high as well. Yes, you will not be doing the daily grind. You may no longer stop in the local pub or party in the club as you once did; however, your costs may not decline. Your cost may just transfer it to something else. Despite going to the

stretchy pant polyester store to buy
your octogenarian clothes, senior
discounts, and early bird specials you
may not save enough to live
comfortably. A major downside with
increasing cost is you do not have the
revenue generated by full-time
employment in your later years to keep
up with cost increases. For those
individuals who do not know, or recall,
inflation in the 1970's soared above
8.5% and in the early 1980's soared
above 13%. What does this mean? The
idea that your retirement may cost you
less on a fixed income or government
subsidies could be a huge mistake.
Protect yourself and invest in your own
financial well-being.   Your best bet
is to accumulate as much as you can
while you can. Have you ever noticed
how squirrels always seem to be
accumulating nuts for the winter? The
squirrels have no idea if it will be a
harsh winter, a mild winter or an
average winter, but that little

squirrel is gathering as many nuts as possible. Be a squirrel. Gather nuts - gather nuts.

Don't Drink Financial Hope-a-Cola. It will rot your teeth, destroy your liver and seriously affect your breathing. Invest in your financial well-being!

✓ **Contributions allowed by government for traditional IRA's and Roth IRA's may vary from year to year. Contributions may also vary based on an individual's age, or marital status. There may also be amounts greater than the allowed contribution as a means to provide individuals the ability to catch up from lack of past contributions. See your certified public accountant, financial professional, or professional tax preparer for further details regarding contributions to Traditional IRAs and Roth IRAs.**

➢ **There are other forms of qualified retirement plans. 403B's and 401K's are a few of the options available** based on occupation and entrepreneurial exploits. As always I encourage individuals to see a financial advisor or certified public account (CPA) for additional information.

I Didn't Forget Social Security

There's still Social Security. It's not that I forgot Social Security; it's just that I really don't rely on Social Security for my retirement security. Debates will continue regarding the health of the Social Security fund for as long as politicians need something to stir the masses. Political dialogue will cause a frenzy for changes regarding when an individual can collect age 62, age 65, age 70 and maybe one day age 75. I prefer to look at Social Security as a supplement, a surprise, an unexpected and welcome gift from an uncle named Sam. The amounts will be manipulated, and change recalculated in order to extend the life of the Social Security program to keep the masses happy. I suppose 30 years from now if I receive a check, I'll say, "great." I have enough to put gas in my car and as I was taught, every little bit helps. This is why I emphasized taking care of your own financial future and not depending on a government to take care of your financial future.

"A government big enough to give you everything you want, is big enough to take away everything you have."
Thomas Jefferson

Question: what happens if all government financial aid provided to our grandparents and parents disappears? What happens if all government financial aid provided to grandparents and parents becomes fiscally miniscule diminishing how they live day-to-day? Be prepared! Help yourself because who's to say, 30 years from now, your Uncle Sam will be able to help you financially?

I implore you please see a financial advisor or a Certified Public Accountant for advice regarding your financial future. It is quite possible with advances in health care you may live well into your late 80's to your early 90's. Do all you can to ensure your money celebrates your four-score and seven years birthday with you!

Transportation

When it comes to transportation, how you get from here to there may vary. Some drive a luxurious car, others drive a truck, some drive a "whoa it's still running," and a select few of us are driven in our limo's by a chauffeur. No matter how you travel the mode of transportation was purchased from someone privately or a dealership. Did you get the best deal? The best deal is one of those subjective things. The best thing you can do is work to get the deal which makes you happy.

Research all venues that highlight

car sales. Play detective and look for deals upon deals and compare. Here are a few suggestions:

- ✓ **Search as many web sites as your eyes can stand before they ache**
- ✓ **Search newspapers**
- ✓ **Search car magazines**
- ✓ **Search free car circular**
- ✓ **Ask friends, family, co-workers**
- ✓ **Bring proof of the car price to the dealership (if a competing dealership advertises a similar car for less via print or the web). Dealerships may be willing to match the price or beat the competitor's price.**
- ✓ **Ask for extras to be thrown in for free (hey, it can't hurt to ask)**
- ✓ **Shop for vehicles during the last week of the month (car dealers and auto sales personnel are looking to make sales goals). They may be a bit more pliable in giving you the price you want.**

✓ **Look at model year leftovers (leftover cars did not sell in their model year). A new 2014 purchased from the dealer in 2015 may be had for a great price.**

✓ **Look at the possible use of a car buying website such as www.truecar.com**

✓ **Prior to personally viewing the car visit www.kbb.com to locate information regarding dealer cost which may help your negotiation**

Car dealerships generally have 87% - 90% of cost built into the car, the rest is pure profit. A $25,000 sticker price would cost the car dealership $21,750. This would provide the car dealerships with a profit of $3,250. The sooner a car is sold by the dealership the greater the profit. Inside scoop - reality - car dealerships finance most of their vehicles with the help of a finance company or bank. They are also on the hook for a monthly payment. The sooner they sell the vehicle the more profit they receive. This is why leftover vehicles can be such a bargain for buyers. The delivery date of the vehicle will let you know how desperate the dealership is to stop making monthly payments on a particular vehicle.

Do not continuously trade in a vehicle. Avoid taking the negative value of your current car to your next car. My cousin Natalie will often do this. She buys a car for $25,000. Three years later she wants a new car and decides to trade her current car. The moment a car is signed, sealed and driven off the dealership's car lot it loses value. The $25,000 car is now worth $22,000 or possibly less. Excessive driving and less than stellar car maintenance (a dent here a dent there, a scratch here a scratch there) have reduced the value of the vehicle. The dealership tells Natalie after evaluating the vehicle it is **upside down**. **Upside down** is a kind way of saying your car is worth less than the amount remaining on your loan. Natalie's car is worth $12,000 but she owes $16,000 after three years of ownership. The difference between what the car is worth and what is owed is called **negative equity (upside down)**. All is not lost just because there's $4,000 in negative equity. The dealer can rollover the negative equity into the purchase of a new car, therefore, a car which has an agreed upon price of $25,000 will be financed for $29,000 ($25,000 + $4000 negative equity). If Natalie does this a few times over her car-buying life, she'll be severely **upside down**.

There's still hope for Natalie. Most car dealerships will emphasize your monthly payment to make a deal work. Normal, car terms are 60 months (five years). Consumers live beyond their means and with a reduction in true cash holdings. Financers of vehicles have become more creative.

They now offer the following loan terms to match those with little cash or bad credit or a combination of both:

✓ **72 months 6 years (Not so bad)**
✓ **84 months 7 years (reaching a bit too far to own a car)**
✓ **96 months 8 years (you may be eating a lot of peanut butter and jelly)**
✓ **108 months 9 years (you're insane if you go through with this deal)**
✓ **120 months 10 years (you're basically buying two cars for the price of one)**

Before you buy a vehicle, create a list of must haves:

✓ **No more than two years old**
✓ **Low miles**
✓ **Efficient use of gas**
✓ **Leather**
✓ **CD player**
✓ **Multimedia connection**
✓ **Bluetooth**

✓ AM/FM

✓ Backup camera

✓ Keyless ignition

✓ Sunroof

✓ Alarm

✓ Good safety rating

The deal isn't over once you've found the car; there's still more to do.

✓ Read the contract before you sign it.

✓ Never sign a blank contract. Common sense, yes but people still do it.

✓ Make sure the interest rate you were quoted is the same as the one on the contract.

✓ Shop around for the best interest rate from the bank, credit union, or the manufacturer of the car.

✓ Be loyal to the interest rate, not the institution.

✓ Make sure you're not buying on impulse, the outfit always looks better in the store than it does at home.

✓ Take a few days to think before you plunk down a ton of borrowed cash.

✓ Consider purchasing an off-lease car (two to three years old), preowned cars that still has years of warranty remaining.

✓ Do not buy a car just because of the German, Italian, or Japanese family name.

✓ You don't need a car that costs more than your rent or mortgage.

✓ Make use of Adam Smith's theory the, "invisible hand of competition"; use it as your ally. If you're set on buying a new or used vehicle, shop around and compare dealership prices. Show the dealers the ads of rival dealerships. Display prices and other deals being offered. Even though you may have a great price, there just might be a dealer willing and able to beat that price. Dealerships may be friendly with each other, but they're friendlier with a customer's cash.

Please take advice from my nephew Malachi. When he was three years old if Malachi saw a Lexus SUV, he'd say "truck." When he saw a Ford Explorer, he'd say "truck." When he saw an Infiniti, he'd say "car."   When he saw a Mercedes Benz he'd say "car." His wisdom was based on limited knowledge and experience, but it makes sense. A car is a car and a truck is a truck. Most of just require transportation to get us where we need to go.

The following chart displays a few vehicles that are related	
Car Company	**Cars they manufacture, own or influences design style**
Honda	Acura
Nissan	Infiniti
Toyota	Lexus
Ford	Lincoln, Mercury, Mazda, Land Rover, Aston Martin

Leasing a car may be a viable option to some. Technically, you don't own the car and there is no equity, but very few people purchase cars for their equity. I know people that change cars every two to three years (cousin Natalie). Consequently, equity and resale value really doesn't matter much to them. They also enjoy the benefit of lower monthly payments and vehicles with the latest features. A deal may be had in demos and off-lease cars, so investigate those options. Car dealerships need to move them out, so you may be able to get one for a song.

In order to add authenticity, I contacted a person I know and trust to get a seller's point-of-view. I went directly to a friend of mine who sells cars for a living. My friend Andre Mannain works for Duchess Cars, a car dealership in upstate New York. Andre has been selling Chrysler, Dodge and Jeep for Duchess Cars for quite some time. I wanted to know, from his perspective, how credit rating and interest rates affected his potential customers on a daily basis. We started off with an exchange of pleasantries and quickly moved to credit. Andre said clearly that the most important thing was a customer's credit score.

Most people that come to the dealership are looking to get a payment around $300 per month. Duchess Cars has a bevy of lenders, somewhere in the neighborhood of 13, they regularly contact in order to acquire financing for a customer's impending purchase. They always try to find the customer the lowest interest rate they possibly can. They will scour their lenders across the nation to find the lowest rate. Based on a customer's credit scores they immediately know which lenders will return an approved response. There are some customers whose credit scores are so bad lenders require a 25% down payment as a condition for financing their loan. When I asked Andre to quantify the credit score with a grade, he asked his co-worker Bill to assist him. The result is a following of an insider's perspective:

- ✓ **750 credit score or greater equals an A or tier 1**
- ✓ **700 credit score to 650 equals a B or tier 2**
- ✓ **650 credit score to 580 equals a C or tier 3**
- ✓ **580 credit score or below equals a D or tier 4**

These ratings apply to purchasing a passenger vehicle and may be different for other items you acquire on credit. I made a recent switch to satellite television service and was afforded a pleasant surprise. The satellite television service checked my credit rating and because of my fairly good credit score, I was provided with free installation. The sales representative said if I had a poor credit score, the installation charges would have varied from $99-$300. It's not just car buying. It's home buying and a plethora of other purchases where your credit score comes into play.

Andre mentioned his vehicle was recently refinanced with our local credit union and based on his good credit, he received a favorable rate. The credit union also provided an additional interest rate discount if he allowed the monthly payment to be withdrawn from his account. The credit union reduced the interest rate by an additional quarter point, saving Andre additional money over time because the interest rate is further reduced.

An individual with a good credit score may actually be able to receive 0% when purchasing a vehicle. Individuals with bad credit scores may pay interest rates as high as 15.9%. Think of it this way, without interest rates an individual car buyer pays $20 per month for every $1,000 that is financed. An individual leasing a vehicle pays on average $200 for every $10,000 that is financed. Now at 15.9% that $20 per month per $1,000 financed increases drastically.

When I asked about the length of car loans, Andre responded by telling me that individuals with good credit generally get loans between 60 and 72 months with interest rates 2.9% through 3.9%. Individuals with bad credit generally pay in the neighborhood of 10.9%, all the way to 15.9%. The norm for a car loan is 60 months. The norm is 72 months, but by far the majority for loans is 84 months. Most of the time young people are getting those 84 months loans, so they can drive the $40,000 vehicle. Recall earlier I mentioned some financial institutions offer 120 month loans (10 years). Older adults will opt for the 60 months when it comes to their loans. It appears as individuals get older, they realize the downside of excess payments, or maybe somewhere along the line they were told about the high cost of finance over a longer period of time.

Purchasing a car is not the end of the story. As the owner the vehicle, you should do everything you can to ensure its longevity. I spoke with another friend of mine, Scott Buley, who also works at Dutchess Cars in their service department. I wanted to provide a real insider input regarding vehicle care. Vehicles are a major investment and should last as long possible. Scott emphasized from the beginning, **"Take care of cars like your grandfather and father took care of their cars."** Scott called it driveway maintenance, basic things you can do to ensure your vehicle runs, runs well, and runs for a very long time.

✓ **Check your fluids**
✓ **Check your tire pressure**
✓ **Do not just leave vehicle maintenance in the hands of other people**
✓ **Read the owner's manual**

✓ **Know how your vehicle operates
understand the workings of the car so
you don't get taken advantage of**

The dealership is located on a 6
mile strip and, according to Scott,
there are 75 places where customers can
take their vehicle for repairs and
maintenance. Dealerships do everything
they can to ensure the customers are
satisfied with the work. He's been into
cars since he was 17 years old. It
helps that he is mechanically inclined
and loves the freedom a car provides.
As a younger man, the distractions of
technology were not as pervasive.
Instead the focus was on the car: to
make the stereo louder, to make the car
faster, more aesthetically pleasing
than the next car. To date, his current
car has 229,000 miles and he expects to
keep his car for 300,000 miles, saving
him a tremendous amount of money over
the life of the vehicle. At the end of
our conversation, I asked Scott what

are three things an individual can do to ensure the life of the vehicle:

- ✓ **timing belt interval**
- ✓ **good tires,**
- ✓ **proper fluid levels**

Take the advice for what it's worth from someone who is in the industry and someone who has a vehicle that's probably running a lot longer than most vehicles on the road. And oh yeah, read your owner's manual.

Sidebar – a breakfast conversation with my niece Ana

An interesting conversation with my niece who is in the process of buying a new car emerged while we were eating breakfast, "What the hell is gap insurance?" she asked "You need it? You don't need it?" A barrage of well-placed questions between sips of her coffee. GAP Insurance (Guaranteed Asset Protection) covers the owner of a vehicle in the event of an accident

that totals their vehicle. GAP will
cover the shortfall between what the
car is valued and what is owed. For
example, the vehicle has an outstanding
loan of $30,000; however, with wear and
tear, mileage and age of vehicle it is
now worth $20,000 based on car industry
standards. In the event of an accident
totaling the car, GAP Insurance would
cover the difference. Therefore, if
your car insurance company only pays
off the $20,000 to your lender, GAP
Insurance will cover the remaining
$10,000. GAP Insurance saved the car
owner from having to find $10,000 they
might not have been able to find. GAP
Insurance's downside: individuals can
spend an extra $750 over the life of
the vehicle and they may never use GAP
Insurance. The $750 will never be
returned to the individual if it is not
used. These days many of the leading
car insurance companies offer GAP
Insurance protection for very little or
absolutely no charge at all in their

insurance package. Purchasing GAP
Insurance from a car dealership may be
redundant and unnecessary.

Why do people trade in cars to car
dealerships if they owe more than the
car is worth? The justification is
simple – they want a new car for
practical or vain reasons.   The car
dealer is more than happy to help the
vain, the practical and the idiot.
Example your trade-in vehicle has an
outstanding loan of $18,000: however,
with wear and tear, mileage and age of
vehicle it is now worth $13,000 based
on car industry standards. If the
dealer had to sell your car, the best
price they could resell the vehicle for
is $13,000 or at least that's what they
say. You agree to buy a new car from
them for $30,000 and they agree to pay
of your upside-down loan. They'll pay
off your car loan of $18,000 and
transfer the negative $5000 to your
brand-new vehicle of choice. Your new

vehicle will have a loan of $35,000 because the $5,000 was added to your $30,000 purchase price.

Home

"I want a house because I have lots of stuff over there and over there and over there…." Justin my precious seven year old

ALL ABOUT THE MONEY

Home ownership is embedded in the American lexicon. The idea of owning one's property to do as one pleases is one of the principles of our culture. In recent times, television has spawned a plethora of renovation, repair, remodel, and diamond-in-the-rough-turned-to-oasis retreats individuals call home. These dwellings may come in different sizes, shapes, colors, structures and styles. Nonetheless, as long as property owners are happy, all is well in their world. So like many of you who enjoy watching The Property Brothers, Flipping Vegas, House Hunters, when the time arrives to commence your search, create your must-have list (what you need and what you would want – bonus items). In addition to dreaming, consider the cost of owning a home. Let's face it even dreams have a price tag.

Here are a few questions you need to ask yourself:

- ✓ What kind of house do I want?
- ✓ How much can I afford to spend (the range of money I can comfortably borrow)?
- ✓ Where do I want to live (school districts, parks, up-and-coming neighborhood, commute to work, public transportation)
- ✓ What kinds of improvements will I have to make (cosmetic changes, fixer upper or money pit)?
- ✓ What is the fair market price (do not overpay because the house was staged)?
- ✓ Is there any wiggle room in the price (are the sellers willing to negotiate)?
- ✓ How much will I need for a down payment (3.5% -FHA Loan, 10% or 20% to avoid PMI)?
- ✓ PMI private mortgage insurance. If the home buyer(s) is/are unable to come up with 20% of the home's appraised value as a down payment, the lender may require PMI mortgage insurance. This will protect the lender if the buyer(s) defaults on the loan.

✓ What is the interest that I will have
   to pay (how's your credit score)?

✓ What mortgage options are available to
   me (fixed, variable and, yes,
   subprime)?

✓ When will you be able to close on the
   home and move in (closing date)?

✓ How much money will be needed at
   closing?

✓ What documents will be needed at
   closing?
   *Acquiring a mortgage (mortgage
   approval will depend and be impacted by
   the following)

✓ Preapproval – prequalified (it's best
   to find out how much money a lender is
   willing to provide before the home
   search begins).

✓ What is your interest rate? This will
   have a direct effect on monthly
   mortgage payments.

✓ What is your monthly payment?

   What are the costs associated with
owning a home? Costs associated with

home buying vary based on where you live. Consult a licensed real estate professional, mortgage specialist to find additional information specific to where you live.

Here are a few items to consider:

✓ Taxes - no one buys a home and gets granted property tax amnesty. Taxes may swing the vote on whether or not you can afford your home.
✓ Title search
✓ Title insurance
✓ Attorney
✓ Appraisal
✓ Rates for a fixed-rate mortgage loan
✓ Rates for an adjustable-rate mortgage loan
✓ Length of mortgage (15 years, 20 years, 30 years)
✓ Length of mortgage is extremely important. The greater the length of the mortgage, the more interests accrues on the principle, which will add to the overall payout for those 30

years. On average, a mortgage of 360 months (30 years) will cost the owner two to three times the amount paid for the house at the closing table. Pete buys a home for $100,000 and has a 30 year fixed mortgage. All things being equal, that final payment will conclude a total payout of over $200,000. That's $100,000 for the house and $100,000 in profit for the bank. Credit score has a lot of say regarding your mortgage payment. A poor credit score, coupled with 360 payments, cost as much as $300,000. That's $100,000 for the house and $200,000 for the bank. One of the ways to shorten the term is to make an extra payment each year. A mortgage with a 30 year life can be reduced to almost a 20-year mortgage with one extra payment per year. That same 30-year mortgage can be reduced even further by making an extra two payments per year. Car buying terms have increased over the last 10 years, going from five years of payments to ten years of payments. There are now mortgage companies, banks and credit unions willing to offer a mortgage for fifty years. The objective is to pay off your home and enjoy your later years. The objective is not to pay off your home and then be placed into a home. Focus on what you really need and what you can really afford. If you can, make an extra mortgage payment or two and enjoy the place that you call home.

✓ Fees (Recording – Transfer)

✓ Credit report

✓ The two most important numbers in your life are your social security number and your credit score. You cannot choose your social security number and you should always protect it. You have great control over your credit score, so manage it properly. If you don't, it's going to cost you when you need it most!

✓ Termite inspection

This does not represent the entirety of

**items which may be considered. Once
again, I urge diligence. Commit
yourself to additional research for a
more exact list.**

Although a mortgage can be
considered a massive debt instrument,
it is connected to an asset (the house
and property it sits on). As the
mortgage decreases over time the home
should appreciate (increase in value)
becoming an extremely important asset.
Additionally, tax benefits may be used
to maintain and improve the property
over time.

**A friendly warning: avoid
repetitive refinancing of your home.
Doing so may come back to haunt you.
When the time to sell your house
arrives, it may be worth far less than
the market is willing to pay for it.
Recall the idea of having a car being
upside down? Well this scenario can
also happen to your home. When your
home is upside down it's considered to**

be underwater.

I recall when I was acquiring my real estate license. My instructor Cathy gave me a bit of advice that I have not forgotten. Cathy said, "If you decide to purchase a model home be careful." Many of us would love to purchase new construction. Newly constructed homes will most likely have a warranty and a reduced amount of unforeseen items which need repair. Models show potential buyers how wonderful their future home could be in order to entice potential buyers. Cathy said based on her 50+ years' experience in the industry, all the data she's read, and heard, model homes have the equivalent of seven years of wear and tear. Although the home may not have existed for seven years, the enormous amount of traffic that has gone through the home, the continuous stream of prospective buyers (and those who are just curious) interacting with the home accumulate to seven years of wear and tear. If you decide to purchase a model home, use this bit of information as a negotiating tool and caveat emptor.

A few words regarding reverse mortgages:

Recall when you decided to purchase a home. You perused through a list of homes, you found a realtor you liked and began house hunting. You went to open houses, weekend after weekend, and finally, you found and bought your home. What if that's the only thing you did in your life that was financially responsible? Retirement approaches or perhaps retirement is here. Either way you are ill-prepared and your only prospect of financial input in your life is Social Security. Fear not – all is not lost.

A possible solution might be selling your house (the thought has

crossed your mind). This would
alleviate financial stress, but perhaps
you would create stress in other areas.
Your saving grace, you paid for your
home for 20 years, 30 years and it's
free and clear or perhaps you're near
the point where it's almost free and
clear and there is minimal debt on your
home. Well, as I stated earlier, your
saving grace may end up being the home
you purchased many years ago. Thanks to
a reverse mortgage. What is a reverse
mortgage? "A reverse mortgage is a
loan for senior homeowners that
uses the home's equity as collateral.
The loan generally does not have to be
repaid until the last surviving
homeowner permanently moves out of the
property or passes away. At that time,
the estate has approximately 6 months
to repay the balance of the reverse
mortgage or sell the home to pay off
the balance. Any remaining equity is
inherited by the estate. The estate is
not personally liable if the home sells

for less than the balance of the reverse mortgage."

http://reversemortgageguides.org/lp/how-does-a-reverse-mortgage-work/?leadint source=GoogleNewReverse&9gtype=content&9gkw=&9gad=47410253697.1&9gpla=mail.google.com&gclid=CNfn4Y20778CFSMV7AodJREAcg

The following items are required in order to qualify for reverse mortgage. However, this small list does not encompass the entirety of the requirements:

✓ **At least 62 years of age**
✓ **Own home free and clear parentheses (homeowners can use money from reverse mortgage to pay off home, making it free and clear).**
✓ **Or home must be lien free (homeowners can use money from reverse a mortgage to pay off liens)**
✓ **Credit scores have little bearing on the acceptance of the home owners qualification for a reverse mortgage**

Once more, I suggest that you see a professional in the industry regarding the possibility of applying for a reverse mortgage to aid with your financial well-being.

"To summarize the key differences with traditional loans the homeowner is still required to make monthly payments, but with a reverse mortgage, the loan is typically not due as long as the homeowner lives in the home as their primary residence and continues to meet all loan obligations. With a reverse mortgage, no monthly mortgage payments are required; however the homeowner is still responsible for property taxes, insurance, and maintenance."

http://reversemortgageguides.org/lp/how-does-a-reverse-mortgage-work/?leadint_source=GoogleNewReverse&9gtype=content&9gkw=&9gad=47410253697.1&9gpla=mail.google.com&gclid=CNfn4Y20778CFSMV7AodJREAcg

A reverse mortgage may be the option which keeps you in the home that you love, living in the neighborhood you love, near the ones you love. A reverse mortgage, coupled with investments, Social Security, and savings may ensure your retirement years are filled with far more ups than downs; more joy than pain and perhaps you may be able to travel to the places you wanted to when you were working 9 to 5 trying to get to this point in your life.

Renters

I have very important advice for those who are not currently in the market for a home. Please purchase renter's insurance. The cost of renter's insurance for an entire year is far less than the cost of your phone or your computer. Individuals can acquire renter's insurance for less than two hundred dollars per year. In addition, Renters Insurance can protect your computer and other specified values. Landlords are not obligated to provide financial compensation to tenants in the event of fire or some other damage to the rental property. The landlord will be far more concerned with their own property. Contact your local car insurance company and ask if they provide renters insurance. You may be pleasantly surprised to find out they do. If all else fails, search the Internet for Renters Insurance and give the various companies you located a call.

"But wait there's more!" Below lists some of the unspoken cost of buying your home.

ALL ABOUT THE MONEY

Our origination charge and/or Lender fees	$0.00
Your credit or charge (points) for the specific interest rate chosen	$0.00
Appraisal	$375.00
Credit Report	$39.00
Flood Certification	$12.00
Tax Service Fee	$96.00
Lender closing attorney fee	$595.00
Lenders Title Insurance	$591.54
Title Endorsements	$125.00
Owners Title Insurance	$596.98
Tax Certificate	$0.00
Other Title Fees APR (POC)	$500.00
Courier Fee	$50.00
Recording Fee	$700.00
County Mortgage Tax/Stamps	$755.40
State Tax/Stamps	$397.58
Attorney Fee- buyer (optional)	$700.00
Total Approximate Cost of Closing Fees	**$5,533.60**

APPROXIMATE COST OF PREPAID INTEREST AND ESCROW/RESERVES	
Interest for 15 days @ $10.99 per day	$164.85
Hazard Insurance HO 6 Condo Insurance	$300.00
Hazard Insurance HO 6 Condo Insurance	$300.00
Mortgage Insurance	$122.76
County Property Taxes	$1,500.00
Total Approximate Cost of Prepaid Interest and Escrows	**$2,387.61**
Total Approximate Cost of Settlement Charges	**$7,921.21**

APPROXIMATE TOTAL OF FUNDS NEEDED TO CLOSE		APPROXIMATE TOTAL MONTHLY PAYMENT	
Purchase Price/Total Liens	$99,395.00	Interest Rate	4.250%
less Earnest Money/Credits	$2,895.00	APR	4.899%
less Total Loan Amount	$94,425.00	Maturity Term 360 mos	30 yrs
less Secondary Financing Amount	$0.00		
less Borrower's closing cost paid by Seller	$0.00	Principal & Interest (or Interest Only payment)	$464.51
plus Mortgage Insurance or Funding Fee	$0.00	Other Financing (P&I)	$0.00
plus Approximate Closing Fees Pd by Borrower	$5,533.60	Real Estate Taxes	$300.00
		Insurance	$25.00
plus Approximate Pre-paid Items/Reserves	$2,387.61	Homeowners Association (if applicable)	$440.00
less Borrower Paid POC Items	$0.00	Mortgage Insurance (if applicable)	$61.38
		Other	$0.00
Total Approximate Funds needed to close	**$9,996.21**	**Total Approximate Monthly Payment**	**$1,290.89**

Down Payment	$4,969.75	5.00%

Basic Savings Tips

"It's much better to date someone who knows how to save money" Yudith Rosario – financial savvy young woman

Basic savings tips:

✓ Bring your own lunch to work as much as possible. If you spend $7.00 per day (not counting snacks throughout the day) and you buy lunch a minimum of four days a week, that's $28.00. Making a sandwich or bringing leftovers will not cost nearly as much. You'll also have time to sit down relax and eat. Less running around like a crazy fool and scarfing down your food may improve your health.

✓ Take a defensive driving class, and save 10% on your car insurance

✓ Donate clothing or other goods to charity and get the receipt; write that amount off when you file your taxes

✓ Give to your religious affiliation; write that amount off when you file your taxes

✓ Return your empty soda and water
  bottles (don't forget your cans)

✓ Donate to your alma matter (send your
  college or university a check and write
  that amount off).

✓ Open an account with a bank that does
  not charge ATM Fees

✓ Buy something during the week from a
  retail store and if it goes on sale the
  following Sunday. Return to the store
  with your sales receipt. They will
  refund the difference between the sales
  price and the price you paid. New York
  grants this rebate (you have a week to
  recover the difference from a purchased
  item that has recently gone on sale).
  Check to see if your state provides the
  same benefit.

✓ Pay yourself first before you pay
  anyone else. Place money in savings, a
  mutual fund, money market account, etc.
  No matter how small, the long-term
  growth achieved makes you glad you did.

✓ Try not to spend your spare change.
  Place it in a jar and cash it in every

**three to four months. I do this before
going on vacation. It's great walking
around money. You will be surprised at**
✓ **how much you will save.**

There may be opportunities to
reduce your income tax burden with tax
deductions as an individual. The
government will allow an individual to
use deductions to reduce their taxable
income. Legally reducing taxable
income will increase the amount of
money an individual will retain for
personal use.

2014 Tax Bracket	
Tax Rate	Single Filers
10%	Up to $9,075
15%	$9,076 to $36,900
25%	$36,901 to $89,350

✓ A single filer with an income of
   $40,000 has a Tax Rate of 25%. Tax
   responsibility (bill) $10,000.$40,000 x
   25% = $10,000

✓ Deductions may reduce the taxable
   amount. For instance if a single filer
   has $3,101 in deductions it will lower
   them into the 15% tax bracket. A
   single filer with an adjusted income of
   $36,899 now has a Tax Rate of 15%. Tax
   responsibility (bill) $5534.84

✓ $36,899 x 15% = $5534.84

✓ $10,000 - $6,000 = $4465.16. That's
   quite a bit of money retained in a
   person's possession.

   I recommend seeing a Certified
Public Accountant (CPA) or licensed tax
preparer, or licensed financial
professional for further details. They
will have far more details as to the
broad array of deductions affecting
individuals, married couples and
businesses. There are additional tax
brackets and scenarios which may better

fit your situation. This serves as an
overview to provide a brief explanation
for the tax novice.

List of possible deductible expenses

- ✓ Advertising
- ✓ Postage
- ✓ Bad debts from sales or services
- ✓ Bank fees on business accounts
- ✓ Education
- ✓ Car and truck expenses
- ✓ Moving
- ✓ Internet (do you use the internet as a required function of your occupation)
- ✓ Commission and fees
- ✓ Depreciation (work related assets or work required assets)
- ✓ Children
- ✓ Dues for trade associations and other not-for-profit business related organizations
- ✓ Employee benefits
- ✓ Telephone

- ✓ Parking
- ✓ Tolls
- ✓ Mileage
- ✓ Gas
- ✓ Gifts to your customers, suppliers, etc.
- ✓ Insurance (casualty and liability)
- ✓ Interest
- ✓ Legal and professional services
- ✓ Meals
- ✓ Entertainment
- ✓ Business dinner
- ✓ Health insurance
- ✓ Medical bills
- ✓ License fees
- ✓ Office expenses
- ✓ Pension and profit sharing plans
- ✓ Publications
- ✓ Rent expense; lease expenses
- ✓ Repairs and maintenance
- ✓ Services performed by independent contractors
- ✓ Supplies and materials
- ✓ Travel expenses

✓ **Utilities**

✓ **Wages of employees**

✓ **And more**

    The IRS will provide the proper forms for all your deductions, but it will depend on the type of business you're running. It may be a Sole Proprietorship, Partnership, Corporation, an Independent Contractor, or Limited Liability Corporation. See a Certified Public Accountant (CPA) or licensed tax preparer, or a licensed financial professional for further details regarding deductible items.

Tips from a professional

    Once more, I decided to contact a professional in the field to aid readers with their future financial decisions. Lucky for me, my college roommate and good friend Craig is a Certified Public Accountant (CPA). When

I contacted Craig he was on vacation.
However, he graciously gave me a few
minutes of his time. I did not want to
take too much time away from his
family, as they were vacationing at
beautiful Niagara Falls. When I asked
Craig what are some of the things an
individual should do regarding their
taxes.

✓ **The first thing he said was file taxes
on time!**

The next thing he told me, was a
good Certified Public Accountants (CPA)
pay for themselves. Sure, you can go to
a national tax preparation chain to
have your taxes prepared, but not so
fast my friend. Think of it this way:
if you met someone who made you flip
head-over-heels and you had only one
date to impress her or him would you to
take them to your favorite fast food
place or your local four-star
restaurant? It becomes a choice
between the place with a dollar menu or

the place with a dress code, a piano in
the corner, candlelight, maître d',
valet parking, and an assortment of
culinary delights. Still unsure? Well
choose the place with The Dollar Menu
and perhaps being served by a kid who's
only working there to pay for a
videogame, phone, or weekend hangout
money will impress your future love.
I'm quite sure all your feelings will
be reciprocated and they will be so
impressed they will now be smitten with
you!

Next, Craig stated it was very
important to keep all your receipts.
It's a lot easier to show your expenses
when you have a record of your
expenses. This led to his next point:
Do not lie on your tax returns. As
the R&B group Jagged Edge sang years
and years ago

You're nothing but
A liar, a cheater, a deceiver, heart
breaker

And I won't let you back in my life
So I'm takin
The house, the cars, the kids, and the
dog
I want it all...

 Jagged Edge

    Well the IRS is not very fond of
you if you're nothing but a liar, a
cheater, and deceiver, and it may lead
to a monetary payout on your part or
jail time. Note: Al Capone did not go
to jail for racketeering, murder, or
other heinous crimes. No, he went to
jail for income tax evasion.

    Whether you're going to a
Certified Public Accountant (CPA) or a
tax preparer you still have a
responsibility to make sure all the
information on your tax returns are
truthful and accurate. Craig said the

signer has the responsibility. Craig
also warned of the **double-child-
claiming.** What's the **double-child-
claiming** you say? This tends to happen
at those national chain tax places
where both parents will claim the child
in the same tax year. Hello people,
that is a major no no! So if one
parent claims the child the other
parent cannot claim the child. Whenever
possible itemize and if it benefits
you, take advantage of it. If you open
your own business, realize that it's a
15% self-employment tax. Don't forget
tax credits. Credits are dollar-for-
dollar reductions in your taxable
amount (some credits are refundable).
This means if you don't owe taxes you
still get a refund. Lastly, take
advantage of your deductions.
Deductions are directly correlated with
whatever tax bracket you fall in.
Before ending our conversation, Craig
emphasized that if you become an
entrepreneur or an investor or your

salary has increased to a large amount, please see a professional better known as a Certified Public Accountant (CPA) to prepare your tax forms. I could no longer hog Craig's vacation time so I thanked him and bid him farewell.

Life 101

Life 101 dictates that no one has a mastery of how life works. There are those who will undoubtedly excel and amass huge fortunes, and those who will battle hardship after hardship in order to reach a level of success. Life 101 does not play favorites. Yet those who are not afraid seek out answers, ask for help and guidance in order to accomplish their goals, and find solutions and information they can implement in their lives.

As I mentioned in my previous book, financial problems or issues do not discriminate. Choose substance over style. Styles change; however substance remains. Substantive materials or substantive individuals have a longer shelf life and perhaps may improve your life situation. The following are some of the common expenditures for most of us if not all.

✓ **Grocery**

ALL ABOUT THE MONEY

✓ **Clothing**
✓ **Furniture**
✓ **Appliances**
✓ **Medicine**
✓ **Travel**
✓ **Phone**
✓ **Dining out**

There is a surefire way to save on groceries. Whenever I went shopping at the local grocery store with my Uncle Gill as a young boy I knew one thing for sure, I was coming home with a full stomach. He'd pack the grill, utensils and seasonings. Once we entered the grocery store, it was off to fruits where he'd immediately sample the apples, oranges, pears, bananas and other fruits. Then off to beverages. He'd pop open a few sodas or juice cans and he'd make me drink milk. Then he'd say, "let's try some of the meat." "Open the grill, boy, and get it started." So, we'd grill some chicken or beef. He would also make me eat some veggies. It was great! We'd have a cookout right there in the supermarket.

At some point the store manager would come to Uncle Gill angry and confused, but Uncle Gill would tell the store manager he would not buy something if he did not like the taste and he's just sampling the food. It was specious reasoning but it worked. He made so much food we'd hand out extras to other customers. After a time, the manger got used to it and just told customers we worked for the grocery store.

No taxation without representation! This is a truism, a rally cry. Well, here's another one: **a person should not buy food that employs sanitation because it has a short expiration!** Don't buy food that spoils quickly. I spend $80.00 to $100.00 every two week without coupons, but when I employ coupons my grocery bill

shrinks. Like a wool sweater in the
dryer, it shrinks. My grocery bill
goes down between, $20.00 and $30.00.
On a few occasions my savings have
crept passed the $30.00 plateau.
Amazing! Putting that in plain
dollars, if you shop every week and
save an average of $25.00 per week you
would save $1,200.00 per year. Could
your family use an extra $1,200.00 per
year?

One more thing if it can be
helped, never ever shop when you're
hungry, depressed and, if you can help
it, leave the children at home.
Children will put things in the
shopping cart and hide them better than
the Easter Bunny hides eggs. Children
are also great at the nag factor and
after 432 **"can I have, can I have…"**
most of us cave-in. Hunger is like that
evil voice in your head saying crazy
things, like

- ✓ "You need those super puffy cheese puffs."
- ✓ "Hey, get one more pack of cookies."
- ✓ "You deserve them."
- ✓ "Come on, you deserve it."
- ✓ "You've been a good girl."
- ✓ "Buy that barrel of doughnuts."
- ✓ "You deserve all these extras."
- ✓ "After all, you got an A in math back in the seventh grade."

Make a list of the items you need. Creating a grocery list is one of the best ways to avoid purchasing items you do not really need at that moment.

Shopping List

DAIRY

☐ Eggs
☐ Milk
☐ Yogurt
☐ Cheddar Cheese

MEAT, FISH

☐ Chicken
☐ Beef
☐ Fish

FRUIT

☐ Bananas
☐ Grapefruit
☐ Grapes
☐ Lemons (yellow)
☐ Limes (green)

VEGGIES S

☐ Broccoli
☐ Lettuce
☐ Mushrooms
☐ Onions
☐ Peppers
☐ Potatoes
☐ Tomatoes

DRY GOODS

☐ Cereal
☐ Oatmeal
☐ Crackers
☐ Pasta/Noodles
☐ Beans
☐ Rice
☐ Flour

BEVERAGE

☐ Coffee
☐ Tea
☐ Fruit Juice

CANNED GOODS

☐ Soup
☐ Spaghetti Sauce
☐ Tuna
☐ Vegetables
☐ Tuna

KITCHEN

☐ Cleaner
☐ Dish Detergent
☐ Glass Cleaner

MISCELLANEOUS

☐ Light Bulbs
☐ Paper Plate

FROZEN FOODS

☐ Orange Juice
☐ Potatoes
☐ Vegetables
☐ Frozen Dinners
☐ Frozen Pizza

BAKING GOODS

☐ Salt
☐ Pepper
☐ Spice

BREADS

☐ Bagels
☐ Bread

CONDIMENTS

☐ Oil
☐ Ketchup
☐ Mayonnaise
☐ Mustard
☐ Pickles
☐ Salsa
☐ Salad Dressing
☐ Honey
☐ Jelly/Jam
☐ Peanut Butter
☐ Syrup

LAUNDRY

☐ Bleach
☐ Detergent
☐ Stain Remover

BATHROOM

☐ Bath Soap
☐ Deodorant
☐ Lotion
☐ Razors
☐ Shaving Cream
☐ Shampoo
☐ Toothpaste

PAPER PRODUCTS

☐ Facial Tissue
☐ Toilet Tissue
☐ Paper Towels

KITCHEN PRODUCTS

☐ Aluminum Foil
☐ Plastic Wrap
☐ Sandwich Bags
☐ Garbage Bags

Hey, I'm Mr. Compliments! "That's a real nice outfit you have on. You always dress so well." You obviously enjoy shopping. Does anyone else enjoy shopping? Some individuals have these simple but time tested shopping rules:

✓ **Have a bad day at work? Go shopping.**
✓ **Feeling bad? Go shopping.**
✓ **Broke up with your boyfriend? Go shopping.**
✓ **Got a new job? Go shopping.**
✓ **Haven't gone shopping in a while? Go shopping.**

Cheap clothing stinks! Let's define cheap before you run off and buy the latest designer goods at some inflated price. Cheap refers to inferior material coupled with poor workmanship used in the making of an outfit or an accessory. If you buy a shirt that is of poor quality, after the first wash or first five minutes and 10 seconds of use, it will disintegrate. Hence the need will arise to purchase another cheap shirt.

Purchasing designer clothing is not all bad. Yet the asking price for certain designer items make me scratch my head and say, "hmm." For instance, I've seen designer underwear for thirty dollars. That's a lot even if you can afford it. Looking fabulous is not determined by the tag or label on a shirt or purse! It's a mental thing. If you think you're fabulous other people will see you as fabulous. Once the mental is in place and you're glowing with, "I'm the stuff dreams are made of attitude," get the outfit to match. Where do you get the designer digs? That's easy.   Outlets!

One of my favorite outlets is the Woodbury Commons Premium Outlets. It features some of the finest brands: Coach, Dolce & Gabbana, Escada, Fendi, Gap, Giorgio Armani, Gucci, Neiman

Marcus, Saks Fifth Avenue, Polo Ralph
Lauren, Prada, Miu Miu, Tod's, Versace,
Zegna, Nike, Timberland and many more
(www.premiumoutlets.com).

If you're saying, "I don't live
near a freaking outlet!" Then perhaps
you live near a closeout store like
Marshalls or T. J. Maxx. Closeout
stores operate like mini-outlets. They
have appliances, pocketbooks, designer
clothing, shoes, jewelry, watches, and
a few surprises. Search the Internet
and locate one near you and go
shopping.

There's another class of closeout
store. The hodgepodge closeout stores
operate like outlet-outlets. They have
electronics, food, giftware, hardware,
furniture, greeting cards, headphones,
flash drives, health and beauty items,
housewares, infant items, lawn and
garden items, sporting goods,
stationery, and toys. Once again, I am
lucky I live near one of the biggest

closeout stores Big Lots! Search the
internet for Big Lots, Ocean State Job
Lot, or ask a friend. They may know of
a place under a different name.

Finally, take a look at thrift
shops especially if the thrift shop is
located in a wealthy neighborhood.
I've been to the Salvation Army in
Manhattan and all I can say is, "Oh
baby!"

**Here's a buying tip; purchase items off
season.**

✓ **Buy winter clothes in the spring,**
✓ **Buy spring clothes in the summer,**
✓ **Buy summer clothes in the fall**
✓ **Buy fall clothes in the winter**

Purchasing clothes at the conclusion
of a retail season can save you 40%,
50%, 60% or more on your apparel. When
it comes to buying for the children,
buy at minimum one size bigger.
Children grow fast and before you know

it the trunk full of cute toddler
clothing you purchased last week no
longer fits your little one. Buy
sturdy play-in-the-dirt clothes, play-
in-the-mud clothes and spilled-juice-
on-my outfit clothing. Buying a
tremendous amount of clothing that is
formal for children may be short-
sighted. Children spend a greater
amount of time playing inside and
outside the house. It's rare that
you'll find a child who will choose to
attend a Broadway show or an opening of
an art gallery over playing outside.
Remember, they're children.

I once had an orange lounge chair.
I really enjoyed my chair with all its
food stains, beverage stains, worn
areas, discoloration, and a few holes.
Unfortunately there came a time when I
had a choice to make, buy a new chair
or rid my home of my orange slumber
machine forever. My chair had become
an eyesore. I chose to rid myself of

the chair. I could have purchased a chair cover for around $25.00 or I could have had the chair reupholstered. All I had to do was put in a little time and a livable solution could have been found.   The new chair was grand, but it did not have the memories and charm of my citrus lounge chair.

Do you need a dresser, entertainment system, dining room table or coffee table? Purchase unfinished furniture. You can finish furniture all by yourself. There may be people who believe that an unfinished table is missing a leg. Well, that's not the case. It just means the table has not been stained. Go to the Home Depot, Lowes or your local hardware store and pick up a can of stain, a brush or two and get to work.

Furniture warehouses can truly be a great place to buy. There's not a lot of fan-fair about these places, but it's the same furniture you'll find in many of the fancy stores. If you cannot find what you're looking for at the furniture warehouse, they might have something comparable or it may be possible to order the furniture you're looking for. Purchase furniture you are comfortable with. Forget fads and trends, it's your money and your furniture should fit your taste. Ignore sneers that may be cast your way by friends and family. Your family and friends sit on their butts not on their face. If your furniture is offensive to someone's tastes tell them to sit on the floor.

Home Depot (and other stores in that genre) sell easy to follow books and CD's, explaining how to fix just about anything, yes even the novice can change an outlet from two prong to three prong. If that's still not your cup of tea, ask your handyman friend, relative or neighbor. It's amazing how motivating a choice beverage and a nice meal can be to some people.

Perhaps the food and beverage swap is not working for you. Well, you can always trade. Here are some possible trades: taxes done for bathroom repair, a roof job for a car tune up, tile the kitchen floor for teeth cleaning and so on.

Question, have you ever gotten sick? Yes. Has your doctor ever prescribed medicine for you? Yes. Ever bought over the counter medicine? Yes. When was the last time you actually compared the store brand to the national name brand? I know you've seen the price difference and it really made no difference in your buying decision unless you were short on funds and desperate. My pharmacist when asked will recommend the generic cold or cough medicine to me. He tells me the only difference is price. I think he's correct. The price and the pride affect whether most people pay for name brand of generic at the cash register. The next time you need a decongestant, read and compare the ingredients between a store brand and national name brand. You'll see little to no difference between the two products (except price).

Travel! When do we leave? Plan to depart on your destination midweek. The end of the week flights are a premium, hence they'll cost you more. Online travel sites are fantastic ways to save. You may also save by going directly to the hotel website, airline website or beach resort website. Cutting out the middle man may save you a few dollars. Those who are not tech savvy may find savings with a travel agent. Times have changed and they must work harder to prove they remain viable. Saving customers some money and having customers spread the word is key for the industry's future existence.

ALL ABOUT THE MONEY

My bill due dates are screwing with me when I get paid. Pick up your phone and call whomever you owe that bill to and ask if it is possible to adjust the payment date so it coordinates with your other bills or pay period. Do this for all your bills. Most companies will do this because if it's easier for you to pay, it's easier for them to collect their money. Not every company or creditor will do this, but the ones that do may just help you align your bills so that a portion of your bills due are when it's best for you.

Why don't you go to cell! Seriously, why don't you cancel the home phone and just use your cell phone. On that note look into noncontract phone plans being offered to save you money. It's not just upstarts that offer noncontract phone plans. These days, the big phone companies are also jumping on the noncontract bandwagon.

Hey, don't eat that! No, it's fine, go ahead eat all you want, but not at their price. There are certain days and times to eat. Restaurants aren't stupid; they know that most folks don't dine midweek, so they'll offer specials.

How do you get these deals? Simply call and ask about midweek deals, there may be deals on drinks, appetizers or meals. One major chain restaurant offers half price appetizers after 10 p.m. and another offers single item unlimited appetizers per person (no sharing). Then, of course, there are coupons. Some are sent in money mailers, Sunday newspapers or those annoying Saturday morning flyers that are piled on your doorstep week after week.

Credit card advantage is in your court

Below is an example of using your credit card in your favor. There I was at Fort Lauderdale Airport heading to the Southwest departure gate when I was politely asked if I had interest in a Southwest Rapid Rewards Premier Credit Card.   I had an hour before my flight was scheduled to depart so I listened to the pitch.

The offer

- ✓ **50,000 points (equivalent two round trips)**
- ✓ **6,000 points on anniversary**
- ✓ **4 Drink coupons (I could use for beer, wine or liquor during flight)**
- ✓ **2 points for every dollar spent**
- ✓ **Periodic emails offering deals for points, products and services**

assenger	Departure/Arrival	Flight	Date
rk Allen	Depart Albany, NY (ALB) on Southwest Airlines at 2:25 PM		Thu Aug 14
			Travel Time 3 h 10 m
	Arrive in Fort Lauderdale, FL (FLL) at 5:35 PM		
rk Allen	Depart Fort Lauderdale, FL (FLL) on Southwest Airlines at 10:55 AM		Mon Aug 18
			Travel Time 3 h 00 m
	Arrive in Albany, NY (ALB) at 1:55 PM		

Price: $12.50 per person, one-wa

Total Cost: $25.0

Thank you Southwest!

The cost of the trip is not a misprint! I flew roundtrip to Florida for $25.00 but I did have to pay the taxes or it would have been a completely free flight.   I use my card for a myriad of purchases continuing to accrue points which I can use for future trips. My role is to be wise and not to overextend myself with poor credit choices.

Conclusion

"Mind what you have learned.

Save you it can."

Master *Yoda*

One of my favorite activities as a teenager was watching the Marx Brothers, although they were way before my time. I enjoy the slapstick comedy and those fantastic one-liners by Groucho Marx.

"While money can't buy happiness, it certainly lets you choose your own form of misery." <u>Groucho Marx</u>

Groucho was absolutely correct. Money doesn't buy you happiness but will take you on a vacation that can cheer you up. Money can pay for the doctor that can fix you up. Money can pay for the condo when you move up. If you're wealthy enough, and you fall, money will pay for someone to pick you up. We live in a world where people pretend that money is not important all the while most people are pretending to have lots of it. Wealthy people will say money isn't everything, and then they enter the luxury car and drive home to a rather nice house or condo. People that don't have money say they're happy without money and having it would only make things more difficult, then they go and buy a lottery ticket. My point is: wealthy, rich, upper middle-class, middle-class, and poor all have discourse regarding money.

"There is only one class in the community that thinks more about money than the rich, and that is the poor." <u>Oscar Wilde</u>

Let's not pretend money doesn't matter. Use money efficiently and invest money wisely, for a better today and fantastic tomorrow!

Thank you for taking the time to

read my book. And remember be about the money all about the money because being poor stinks. If not having money to live a fairly decent life doesn't stink, then the smell is slightly obnoxious.

Sincerely, Kirk Allen.

Shopping List

DAIRY

- ❑ Eggs
- ❑ Milk
- ❑ Yogurt
- ❑ Cheddar Cheese

MEAT, FISH

- ❑ Chicken
- ❑ Beef
- ❑ Fish

FRUIT

- ❑ Bananas
- ❑ Grapefruit
- ❑ Grapes
- ❑ Lemons (yellow)
- ❑ Limes (green)

VEGGIES S

- ❑ Broccoli
- ❑ Lettuce
- ❑ Mushrooms
- ❑ Onions
- ❑ Peppers
- ❑ Potatoes
- ❑ Tomatoes

DRY GOODS

- ❑ Cereal
- ❑ Oatmeal
- ❑ Crackers
- ❑ Pasta/Noodles
- ❑ Beans
- ❑ Rice
- ❑ Flour

BEVERAGE

- ❑ Coffee
- ❑ Tea
- ❑ Fruit Juice

CANNED GOODS

- ❑ Soup
- ❑ Spaghetti Sauce
- ❑ Tuna
- ❑ Vegetables
- ❑ Tuna

KITCHEN

- ❑ Cleaner
- ❑ Dish Detergent
- ❑ Glass Cleaner

MISCELLANEOUS

- ❑ Light Bulbs
- ❑ Paper Plate

FROZEN FOODS

- ❑ Orange Juice
- ❑ Potatoes
- ❑ Vegetables
- ❑ Frozen Dinners
- ❑ Frozen Pizza

BAKING GOODS

- ❑ Salt
- ❑ Pepper
- ❑ Spice

BREADS

- ❑ Bagels
- ❑ Bread

CONDIMENTS

- ❑ Oil
- ❑ Ketchup
- ❑ Mayonnaise
- ❑ Mustard
- ❑ Pickles
- ❑ Salsa
- ❑ Salad Dressing
- ❑ Honey
- ❑ Jelly/Jam
- ❑ Peanut Butter
- ❑ Syrup

LAUNDRY

- ❑ Bleach
- ❑ Detergent
- ❑ Stain Remover

BATHROOM

- ❑ Bath Soap
- ❑ Deodorant
- ❑ Lotion
- ❑ Razors
- ❑ Shaving Cream
- ❑ Shampoo
- ❑ Toothpaste

PAPER PRODUCTS

- ❑ Facial Tissue
- ❑ Toilet Tissue
- ❑ Paper Towels

KITCHEN PRODUCTS

- ❑ Aluminum Foil
- ❑ Plastic Wrap
- ❑ Sandwich Bags
- ❑ Garbage Bags

All About Glossary

Investors often speak a different language. The words used can often confuse individuals not accustom to the language of investing. I hope I have not continued this practice of confusing individuals with my choice of words. Cavalier use of financial language without some explanation does not benefit anyone. In an effort to pass information on I created a glossary of terms which may help with financial endeavors by you the reader.

401K - A tax-deferred savings plan allowing an employer to match an employee's deposits into an account up to 100%.

403B - A tax-deferred savings plan

for government and non-profit employees allowing an employer to match an employee's deposits into an account up to 100%.

Annual Percentage Rate (APR) – The yearly interest rate charged on a credit account.

Annuity - A clearly expressed financial amount payable to account holder for a stated period of time.

Asset Allocation – The processes of using numerous investment vehicles to spread risk among various investment vehicles.

Bear – An individual (investor) who believes the market, a targeted security of targeted industry will have an upswing.

Blue Chip Company - A company with a trustworthy financial history and sustained growth.

Bond - A promise to repay a borrower a fixed amount at a specified future date. Bonds are usually sold at a discount. Bonds are sold by federal government, state government and municipalities. Corporations also offer bonds for sale to the general public.

Borrower - A person who uses a lenders, creditors or financial institution's money for their own purpose. Interest is charged on the borrowed amount to earn profit.

Bull – An individual (investor) who believes the market, a targeted security of targeted industry will have a downswing.

Call Option – The investor purchases a commodity with the belief the commodity will increase in price.

Capital Gains - Increased value of a security at redemption based on the original amount invested (principal) increasing.

Certificate of Deposit (CD) - A saving instrument acquired for a definite dollar amount providing a fixed amount based on a fixed interest rate for a targeted date.

Commission - The payment to a financial representative (stockbroker) or agent for carrying out a financial transaction.

Common Stock - Securities representing equity ownership in a public company.

Compound Interest - Interest earned on principal plus previously accrued interest.

Consumer – An Individual who uses personal financial holdings to obtain goods or services.

Credit Score – A person's history of credit usage (debt paying, outstanding loans) are computed to calculate their credit score. A credit score ranges between 300 and 850. Individuals with high credit scores (725 and above) are considered credit worthy and are far more likely to repaid the loan.

Diversification - A strategy intended to minimize risk by distribution investment money among a number of investment types and industries.

Dividend - Money paid to owners of stock by corporations.

Dollar Cost Averaging - Investing a fixed-dollar amount regularly in an investment over a long period of time.

Dow Jones Industrial Average (DJIA) - A market indicator comprised of several blue chip stocks in varying industries.

Economy - A system of financial interactions based on the decisions of buyer and sellers.

Federal Deposit Insurance Corporation (FDIC) - the government agency created to guarantee depositors funds.

Financial Adviser - A professional providing financial advice and allocating pertinent financial information to clients or potential clients regarding their financial goals. Financial advisers may include accountants, insurance agents, or attorneys

Financial plan – A written or verbal plan outlining an individual's financial goals.

Futures – A contract to buy or sell an exact amount of a commodity at targeted future date and price.

Futures Contract place an obligation on the buyer to purchase an asset or the inverse a seller to sell an asset.

Income – Money obtained by an individual because of investments or work.

Individual Retirement Account (IRA) – A government savings plan allowed promoting savings for retirement.

Inflation – A broad spectrum rise in costs of goods and services. Generally money's purchasing power decreases.

Insurance – The risk taken on by a company for a fee (premium). The insured is afforded protection based on payments of cash to a company.

Interest Rate – The basic cost associated with borrowing money. The lender charges interest and the borrow pays interest.

Interest Rate – A percentage levied on the principal amount as means of making money for the lender.

Investing – An individual's personal funds used to increase financial wellbeing. The risk taken is not a promise of financial gain or expectation of financial loss.

Investment Adviser – A professional providing financial advice and allocating pertinent financial information to clients or potential clients regarding their financial goals.

Investment Plan – A written or verbal plan outlining an individual's financial goals.

Lender – An organization or individual that provides funds to a borrow in order to make a profit.

Liabilities – The dollar value of all

debts owed by an individual.

Liquidity – The quickness and ease that an individual can convert investments to cash.

Load Fund – Mutual funds that have sales charges and commissions (also known as loads).

Management Fees - The financial charges place on mutual fund investors to maintain the mutual funds.

Markets – a financial meeting place for buyers and sellers to exchange possessions.

Matching Contribution – The amount of money an employer contributes to an employee's retirement plan.

Mutual Fund Fees (12B-1 Fees) – The financial charges allocated to investors to cover the various costs of sustaining a mutual fund.

Mutual Fund – An investment based on diversification and professional management of investor funds.

National Credit Union Association (NCUA) - The federal organization that protects depositor's funds.

Net Worth – An individual's actual accounting of their personal value based calculating all their assets owned and then subtract all their liabilities.

New York Stock Exchange (NYSE) – The granddaddy of all stock exchanges in the United States.

No-Load Fund – A mutual fund that general skips the middle man and is purchased from the fund company avoiding the sales charge.

Opportunity Cost – The act of choosing one thing for another. The value one gives up for the alternative good or service.

Pay Yourself First – The act of paying yourself a set dollar amount before anyone or institution. Pay yourself first into an investment vehicle!

Portfolio – The range of interments held by a person or corporation.

Precious Metals – Minerals such as gold used as an investment vehicle.

Preferred Stock - A form of stock which provides rights to company assets before common stock holders. Owners of common stock are also provided a dividend.

Price - The price of good or service based on market forces.

Principal - The initial amount of money invested.

Prospectus (legal document) - Relevant Information provided to the general public as means of aiding potential investors regarding thoughts of investing in a particular company.

Public Company - A business entity which has shares of ownership (stock) available to the public at large.

Put Option - The investor purchases a commodity with the belief the commodity will decrease in price

Real Estate - Property obtained as a measure of investment (business, rental, or personal property).

Return - The return of funds in excess of what the individual has invested (minus fees and capital gains taxes).

Risk - The chance an investor will not profit from investing.

Risk verses Return Quandary - The idea which proclaims greater risk equates to greater rewards.

Risk Tolerance - The amount of risk an individual is willing to take on when investing.

Rule of 72 - A brilliant but simple way of determining the interest rate or future years required to double a person's money.

Savings - Money not used for needs and wants usually held in a financial institution.

Savings Account - An account for savings money that often pays low interests but offers superior security for a customer's money.

Securities and Exchange Commission (SEC) - A federal agency responsible for governing the securities industry and enforcing securities laws.

Simple Interest - Basic amount levied on

a borrower for the access to money.

Securities Investor protection Corporation (SIPC) - An independent organization that acts as trustee to recover assets of customers if a brokerage firm goes out of business.

Stock - Ownership in a company that can be bought, sold or retained in the hopes of increased value.

Stockbroker - A licensed financial representative, who buys, sells and offers advice to customers in the stock market.

Stock Market - The place where buyers and sellers of stock meet to complete stock transactions (buying and selling stock).

Stock Symbol - A set of letters representing a specific stock, mutual fund, or other security. Sometimes referred to as a ticker symbol.

Tax-Deferred - Money invested that is taxed when it is withdrawn.

Salutes

First I want thank God for helping me complete this project. Grandma, thank you for believing in me, encouraging me, and being an unbelievable role model. Mom Heintz, thanks for the love, guidance, support and letting me drive home after one of my college visits. Paul, always stay active and can I please have a Pepsi now? Kes thanks for being so patient throughout the creation of this book. Uncle Tony this one is for you, I hope you enjoy reading this. Ty you did (you beat cancer (twice)! Justin keep smiling (very proud of you). Oneonta State University, Western Connecticut State University thanks for not wasting my time (really). Writing this book was truly a labor of love. Andrew thanks for being my brother's keeper

since the days of way back (Just-Ice).
Greg Hanson I owe a lot of this to you,
thanks. Noemy thank you for all the
encouragement over the years, even when
things looked so bleak you stayed
positive. Pete, O-state, connection is
still strong after all these years.
Uncle D.V. thanks for all the great
advice (keep riding in the sun).
Cherly Peeters you're simply the best –
always there whenever I reach out (I
would not be here without you).
Shannon you're an incredible friend.
Thank you for introducing me to clay
(and worm art)! Venus thanks for the
stern looks. Lou you're a real cool
dude with great stories. Rahjer T.
keep climbing that mountain I know
you'll make it to the top (sky's the
limit). Greg B. thanks for allowing me
to take my cover pictures in the
restaurant club. Bo Whaley thanks for
scaring the hell out of me from day
one. Dr. Omara I appreciate all the
knowledge you passed on to me. Sean

thanks for including me in your project (The Brothers of The Black List). The next book is on the way Dr. Meanor! My family and friends thank you for all your support. Last but not least I want to express my profound thanks to all the people that read this book. I hope it helps you as much as possible.

Special thanks to my friends of yesteryear. We were once "Starters" and have remained so through all of our ups and downs of life. We root for each other as young men and continue to root as grey hairs invade our heads. One day I hope to tell our wild stories so our children can read about our great silliness, pain, moments of weakness and triumphs. I hope one day we will all look back and say we were also "Finishers!"

Forever Starters: Andrew, Joel, Ydde, Shawn, Vinny, Scott, Donald (R.I.P.), Keith, Rashan, and Derreck.

ALL ABOUT THE MONEY

Special thanks my niece Ana. Anna, you're crazy-cool, thank you for all your help. I am very lucky to have a niece who I can call on for help.

Hey - Nick I didn't forget you. Thanks for providing me with a smooth haircut.

Anjary – Your cover photo is Amazing. Your picture ads so much to the book! Thank you very much!!!

Online References

http://www.creditdonkey.com/no-emergency-savings.html

http://www.cbsnews.com/news/shocking-number-of-americans-have-no-retirement-savings/

http://blogs.wsj.com/wealth/2010/09/07/the-perfect-salary-for-happiness-75000-a-year/

http://www.gettingacreditcard.com/article57.shtml

Daniel P. Ray and Yasmin Ghahremani
http://www.creditcards.com/credit-card-news/credit-card-industry-facts-personal-debt-statistics-1276.php

http://www.aie.org/managing-your-money/credit-cards/The-True-Cost-of-Credit-Cards-A-Repayment-Table.cfm

http://planit.cuna.org/015111/article.php?doc_id=40

http://money.usnews.com/funds/mutual-funds/large-blend/vice-fund/vicex

http://money.usnews.com/funds/mutual-funds/large-blend/vice-fund/vicex

Dr. Don Taylor, Ph.D., CFA, CFP, CASL
http://www.bankrate.com/finance/credit/credit-score-interest-rates.aspx

www.experian.com

www.transunion.com

www.annualcreditreport.com

www.consumer.gov/Idtheft

http://reversemortgageguides.org/lp/how
-does-a-reverse-mortgage-
work/?leadint source=GoogleNewReverse&9
gtype=content&9gkw=&9gad=47410253697.1&
9gpla=mail.google.com&gclid=CNfn4Y20778
CFSMV7AodJREAcg

www.truecar.com

www.kbb.com

www.premiumoutlets.com

Before I Let You Go

When it comes to your financial
life do not follow, do not get out of
the way. You must take the lead!
You've all heard "life is not fair!"
So what! Move on and create a plan of
action to have a successful financial
life. You could be a butcher, a baker,
a candlestick maker and have a
successful, joyous and financial stable
life.

As a child I watched cartoons, and one
of my favorite characters was Scrooge
McDuck. He was a meticulous money
manager (obsessed more than most with
his personal finances) who knew where
every penny was and still has the first
dime he ever made. Scrooge McDuck said
something I held as profound wisdom,
"Work smarter not harder!"

If you desire to have a financial life with less upheaval, and without tidal waves of debt, a hellish credit score, ridiculous car payments, inadequate life insurance (or no life insurance) and a host of other financial issues, this book seeks to help you.

Locate a financial advisor or Certified Public Accountant whether it be through a family member, friend, co-worker, or your own diligent searching to aid in customizing a plan for your financial life.

About the Author

I have always had a thirst for knowledge which has taken me along this path; University of The West Indies (teacher online), New York State Business Teacher for nearly two decades; Leadership Academy Certification- Massachusetts College of Liberal Arts (2010); Masters Western Connecticut State University graduate Instructional Technology (2002); I am a two time graduate of the State University at Oneonta; Bachelors of Science Business Economics (May 1995), Bachelors of Science Business Education (1997); Chrysler Finance (auditor); Livingston International (custom broker), First Investors (Registered

Representative); Primerica (Independent Representative); K-Fortuna (License Real Estate Agent).   I am also a Veteran of the United States Military. At some point in my life I held the following licenses: Series 6, Series 63, Series 3 Life and Health Insurance and my bartender's license.

No matter the breath of my experience and education, I never walk into a room thinking, "I am the smartest guy in the room." However, I have left that very same room pleased to know I left knowing more than I did when I entered.

My financial aptitude was forged early in life by poverty and an incredible woman (my grandmother) who provided insightful financial lessons encompassing needs and wants. Saving was emphasized over spending. A strong financial today was a constant song in the house. Tomorrow may never come but if you wake up in the morning, tomorrow

has arrived and you need to be prepared
to meet it. Teachings of mindful
spending remain embedded in my head to
this very day. Life lessons never die;
they get passed on to a next life and a
next life for a better existence.

I did not want time to erode my
future ability to relax and enjoy life.
The zero guess is a real life changer
and has necessitated financial tactics
to attain. Realizing zero, will
alleviate stress issues and problems
all related to money in my life. Zero
will equate to lessons learned, lessons
practiced and victory. I enjoy finance
because it is a game changer. Life has
so much to offer and limited resources
may limit the experience. As I said
before, money is not a be all and end
all, but is a help all. I will
continue to express these ideas,
lessons and information enabling
individuals to implement them into
their own lives. I once heard a little
bit goes a long way - well let's see

how far you can take. Here's what I
know, if you're reading this you're on
your way!